Buddhism
in the
West

CONTRIBUTORS TO
BUDDHISM IN THE WEST

Michael Toms and His Holiness the Dalai Lama

Thich Nhat Hanh   Robert Aitken Roshi   Kalu Rinpoche

Robert Thurman

Lama Tulku Thondup Rinpoche

Stephen Batchelor

Tai Situpa Rinpoche

Lama Surya Das

Jack Kornfield

Quotes about Michael Toms

"...one of the best interviewers who has ever worked the American airwaves, radio, or TV."
— Robert Fuller, physicist, educator, past president of Oberlin College, and chairman of Internews, Inc.

"Someone with whom I have cruised some important realms of the cosmic ocean and in doing so have developed ever-increasing confidence in his intuitive navigation."
— R. Buckminster Fuller (1895–1983), inventor of the geodesic dome; designer, philosopher, and creator of the World Games

"...Bill Moyers and Michael Toms are alike: two of the most creative interviewers it has been my good fortune to work with."
— Joseph Campbell (1904–1987), mythologist and author of *Hero with a Thousand Faces, The Masks of God, Myths to Live By,* and *The Mythic Image*

"In my experience, you are the best interviewer in the world (and having been interviewed in over 35 countries, I speak with authority). Your questions are so deep, showing true inner knowledge and reflective understanding of the issues your interviews are raising, and you provide so warm and yet so focused a set and setting for the interview that you create a context in which we begin to understand what one is really about."
— Jean Houston, Ph.D., author of *A Mythic Life* and *A Passion for the Possible*

"I have always admired Michael's ability to synthesize complicated ideas and get to the heart of the matter. He is creative and imaginative with an enthusiasm that comes from truly understanding the material and applying it in his own life."
—Charles Garfield, Ph.D., clinical professor at the University of California, San Francisco School of Medicine; author of *Peak Performers;* and co-author of *Wisdom Circles: A Guide to Self-Discovery and Community Building in Small Groups*

❖❖❖

Please visit the Hay House Website at: **www.hayhouse.com**
and the New Dimensions Website at: **www.newdimensions.org**

Buddhism
W in the est

Spiritual Wisdom
for the 21st Century

The Dalai Lama
Tai Situpa Rinpoche
Thich Nhat Hanh
Stephen Batchelor
Kalu Rinpoche
Robert Aitken Roshi
Jack Kornfield
Lama Surya Das
Lama Tulku Thondup Rinpoche
and
Robert Thurman

with Michael Toms

Hay House, Inc.
Carlsbad, CA

Published and distributed in the United States by:
Hay House, Inc., P.O. Box 5100, Carlsbad, CA 92018-5100
(800) 654-5126 • (800) 650-5115 (fax)

Edited by Michael Toms, Rose Holland, and the Hay House editorial staff
Introduction, Prologues, and Epilogues by Michael Toms
Designed by Highpoint, Inc., Claremont, CA

The authors of this book do not dispense medical advice or prescribe the use of any technique as a form of treatment for physical or medical problems without the advice of a physician, either directly or indirectly. The intent of the authors is only to offer information of a general nature to help you in your quest for emotional well-being and good health. In the event you use any of the information in this book for yourself, which is your constitutional right, the authors and the publisher assume no responsibility for your actions.

Library of Congress Cataloging-in-Publication Data

Buddhism in the West : spiritual wisdom for the 21st century / contributors, The Dalai lama . . . [et al.] ; with Michael Toms.
    p.   cm.
    ISBN 1-56170-505-5 (alk. paper)
    1. Religious life—Buddhism. 2. Buddhism—Doctrines.
I. Bstan-'dzin-rgya-mtsho, Dalai Lama XIV, 1935– II. Toms, Michael.
BQ4302.B84   1998
294.3'09182'1—dc21

                                    97-41203
                                      CIP

ISBN: 1-56170-505-5

01 00 99 98   5 4 3 2
Second Printing, July 1998

Printed in Canada

New Dimensions Radio® is a registered trademark of New Dimensions Foundation.

Contents

❖❖❖

Editor's Note: Throughout this book, the
interviewer's questions are in italics.

PREFACE

About New Dimensions

New Dimensions Radio is the major activity of the New Dimensions Foundation, a nonprofit educational organization. "New Dimensions" is an international radio interview series featuring thousands of hours of in-depth dialogues on a wide variety of topics. **Michael Toms,** the co-founder of New Dimensions Radio, the award-winning host of the "New Dimensions" radio interview series—and a widely respected New Paradigm spokesperson and scholar himself—engages in thoughtful, intimate conversations with the leading thinkers and social innovators of our time, focusing on creative and positive approaches to the challenges of a changing society.

About This Book

During the past two decades, we have been afforded the opportunity to speak with many of the Buddhist teachers who have traveled from Asia to the West, as well as those Westerners who have emerged as Buddhist teachers in their own right. This book presents several of the major figures from different schools of Buddhism, including the Tibetan, Zen, and Theravasdin (Vipassana) approaches as presented by both Eastern and Western teachers. The commonsense approach inherent within Buddhist ideals is very compelling to those of us living in the West because it appeals to our practical, down-to-earth orientation. The Buddha emphasized the importance of direct experience. Follow the precepts because they work for you, not because you're supposed to follow them.

The simplicity and straightforward directness of Buddhism comes through as you read the words of those included in this volume. May their voices benefit your life and all life on the planet.

❖❖❖

INTRODUCTION

Surveys and polls indicate that a greater and greater number of people are becoming more interested in the spiritual domain. Workers are seeking more meaning and purpose in their livelihoods. Meditation has entered the mainstream. Spiritually related books dominate the bestseller lists. All this is by way of explaining why the 2,500-year-old tradition of Buddhism has taken the West by storm. Buddhism is said to be the fastest growing religion and one of the most influential spiritual movements in North America and Europe. It has become clear that Buddhism is playing a significant role in the new planetary culture and one quite different from the usual East–West encounters of the past.

In 1989, **his Holiness the Dalai Lama** of Tibet was awarded the Nobel Peace Prize, and this served to further popularize Buddhism in the West. This book begins with the Dalai Lama speaking about what Buddhism can contribute, and the value of its explanation of existence. Following his Holiness is the venerable **Tai Situpa Rinpoche**, one of the Vajra Regents in the Kagyu school of Tibetan Buddhism, who expresses the nonviolent nature of Buddhist philosophy. **Thich Nhat Hanh,** in his inimitable fashion, gently leads us into nonself, impermanence, and the wonders of mindfulness. **Stephen Batchelor** gives us a sense of Buddhist history and its impact on various Asian countries as well as the West. The late **Kalu Rinpoche** (whose reincarnation has been identified in India) opens the door to the nature of mind and the importance of love and compassion. **Robert Aitken Roshi** addresses the pragmatic relevance of Buddhist precepts and how they can enable us to meet the challenges of daily life. The practice of lovingkindness underscores American Buddhist **Jack Kornfield's** approach. Another American, **Lama Surya Das**, reminds us that we are all Buddhas by nature and provides insights to help us live that wisdom. **Tulku Thondup Rinpoche** points out that each of us possesses an astounding power to heal ourselves emotionally and physically, and this power resides in our minds. The book concludes with scholar and former monk **Robert Thurman** providing a marvelous overview of the origins, evolution, and philosophy of Buddhism and the importance of supporting the Tibetans and their human rights relative to China's occupation of Tibet.

— Michael Toms
Ukiah, California
January 1998

❖❖❖

CHAPTER ONE

The Power of Compassion

The Dalai Lama and Michael Toms

PROLOGUE

His Holiness Tenzin Gyatso, 14th Dalai Lama in a line of incarnate Buddhist monarchs dating back to the 14th century, is a modern spiritual leader who manifests an acute awareness and concern for contemporary social issues. Born to a peasant family, his Holiness was recognized at the age of two, in accordance with Tibetan tradition, as the reincarnation of his predecessor, the 13th Dalai Lama. The Dalai Lama is the political, religious, and spiritual leader of the Tibetan people.

Unlike his predecessors, his Holiness has traveled extensively in the Western world, meeting with major religious and secular leaders in Western Europe, North America, the Soviet Union, and Asia. During his travels abroad, his Holiness has spoken strongly for better understanding and respect among different faiths. He has made numerous appearances at interfaith services, imparting the message of universal responsibility, love, compassion, and kindness. Since his first visit to the West, his Holiness's reputation as a scholar and a man of peace has grown steadily. Western universities and institutions have conferred peace awards and honorary doctoral degrees upon him in recognition of his distinguished writings and Buddhist philosophy, and for his leadership in the service of freedom and peace.

On October 5, 1989, his Holiness was awarded the Nobel Peace Prize. The Nobel committee stated that "the Dalai Lama . . . consistently has opposed the use of violence. He has instead advocated peaceful solutions based upon tolerance and mutual respect." To Tibetans, the Dalai Lama is the embodiment of their faith, the symbol of their national identity, and their hope for freedom. To the rest of the world, his Holiness is a devoted and highly respected advocate of universal compassion, justice, and peace.

Shortly before receiving the Nobel Peace Prize, his Holiness visited Central America and Costa Rica for the first time and participated in the first major interfaith gathering ever to be held in Central America. He was a keynote speaker along with President Oscar Arias of Costa Rica, also a Nobel Peace Prize laureate, at the "Seeking the True Meaning of Peace" conference. It was during this conference that I had the rare opportunity to have a private interview with his Holiness, at a convent of Catholic nuns where he was staying outside of San Jose, Costa Rica.

❖❖❖

MICHAEL TOMS: *What are your impressions of Costa Rica?*

THE DALAI LAMA: What I have seen of the country itself is very beautiful. Its people, it seems, are not rushing as in New York and other places. This country has no military forces, no production of military equipment. These things, I think, are very important, as everyone talks about peace and disarmament, trying to reduce arms production, and arms competition. I really was impressed when they instituted this practice in the '40s. At that time, I saw no one else practicing this kind of idea. And also, you see, things were very complicated at that time, in the 1940s and 1950s, during World War II. So I am very impressed. And I feel that we could learn many things from this country's experience.

What do you think Buddhism offers people that live in these times? What do you think that Buddhism brings to us today?

I believe that Buddhism, as with any other religion, has some potential to contribute—mainly through mental peace and by changing our outlook on life in terms of our neighbors and our environment. So that, I think, is what Buddhism can contribute. One special significance of Buddhism is the theoretical explanation of existence. Things are relative. Things are interdependent. That is a very helpful way to look at the world. For example, the modern economic structure itself is a very good example of interdependency, isn't it? It is heavily interdependent. I was at lunch the other day with the Archbishop of this country, and he mentioned that they produce bananas here and sell them to the United States. And this country buys U.S. wheat. It is an exchange; things are dependent on one another.

Another aspect of Buddhist philosophy that I think has some special significance is the idea of things being relative. God is always found somewhere between black and white or between negative and positive. You cannot say, "This is my enemy," and see that enemy as 100 percent negative. Nor can you say, "This is my friend," and see the friend as 100 percent positive. That is impossible. Basically, this is the same situation. It is that kind of attitude that is very helpful in reducing hatred. I always say, "Talk to people." Religious people should not think only of how to propagate their religion, but also of how much they can contribute to humanity.

How do you see the connection and the relationship between Buddhism and Christianity here and in the rest of the Western world?

Generally, the relationship among various religions during the last few years is much improved—particularly between Tibetan Buddhism and Christianity. They have a much closer relationship; a much deeper understanding has developed. The present Pope and I have had several occasions to discuss this. And I've also discussed this with many other important figures in the Catholic and Protestant communities. I think we've developed very positive, close relationships. And that is very helpful to mutual learning. We have learned many things from Christian tradition that are very useful, very practical. At the same time, our Christian brothers and sisters also learned some new techniques from us. For example, there is the practice of love and compassion and forgiveness. There is also a certain Buddhist technique adopted or utilized that involves concentration, or discipline. It is the Shamata—the one-pointedness of mind. That practice in Buddhism, in Eastern philosophy, is still a living tradition. It is something that I think is useful for some of our Christian practitioners.

In 1968, Thomas Merton came to Asia on his first visit out of the States. You had a chance to meet with him. He was a Catholic Trappist monk who was very interested in Tibetan Buddhism. What do you remember of your meeting with Thomas Merton?

That was a very pleasant meeting. And also, due to meeting with him, my understanding of Christianity was expanded, adding to my genuine respect for Christian practitioners and their contribution to humanity. I consider Thomas Merton a very strong, solid bridge between East and West. Since his sudden death, I've felt a great loss. I think he made one big contribution regarding a closer understanding and relation between Christians in general—and Catholics in particular—and Tibetan Buddhists.

You have spoken about compassion and love producing an inner courage and inner peace. Could you explain?

Compassion is a concern for people—for other sentient beings. And it is not merely a feeling of sympathy and pity, but a desire to do something to help. That is the kind of compassion that opens one's mind and one's self to others. It automatically develops a feeling that the other is part of you. And I think that helps. You see, there is no barrier; fear and suspicion are reduced. That, in turn, gives you courage and will.

Many people feel overwhelmed and oppressed when they look at the external world and its many problems. They feel unable to do anything. How can one small individual make a difference in a world with so many problems? What do you have to say to that?

Today's problems did not spring up overnight. It could be anywhere from two years to two centuries that brought these problems where they are today. So now, the issue is to reduce or eliminate our problems, which may also take 100 years. It takes time; that's the nature of change. Basically, many of these negative things are essentially man-made. If we do not want these things to exist, we have to make an effort to change them. No one else is here to take care of them. We have to face them ourselves. There is no other choice. But the initiative must come from the individual. First there is one individual, then another joins, then a third person joins, until there are 100, then 1,000. After all, human society, human community, means a group of individuals. A big change will not take place because of one individual effort, but by the combined efforts of individuals.

How do you see what went on in China in June 1989 in relation to what has been going on in Tibet? How do you see the future of Tibet relative to that unrest?

For the time being, because the Chinese government practices hard-line policy, it is Tibetan policy, too. But there is something else going on in China. Something really great, I think, of historical importance. One thing that impresses me is that although the Chinese people—particularly the students—are brought up and educated in the communist society, which is of a violent nature, the people sincerely and strictly follow Mahatma Gandhi's teachings of nonviolence. That is something really remarkable. This is a kind of confirmation, for me, that nonviolence is much closer to basic human nature, or human spirit, than is generally credited.

They were completely nonviolent in their demands for more freedom, more democracy, and less corruption. That, also, I think, is very beautiful. And although for the time being they lost, I think they made a great impact in the Chinese people's mind and on the world outside, too. Because of their strong human spirit and sincere motivation, it is only a question of time, I think, until their wish will be fulfilled. And I pray for their goal. China is the most populated nation in the world. As a Buddhist monk, when I pray for all sentient beings, that means a greater part of my prayer includes China because it has the largest population. Even small things can have a big effect in that country, because it affects so many people—more than a billion human souls.

❖❖❖

MICHAEL TOMS: That interview took place with the Dalai Lama in Costa Rica in June 1989. In October 1989, his Holiness led the chanting during the performance of a traditional Tibetan Lhasang ceremony designed to heal the environment. This ceremony was performed atop Mt. Tamalpais in Marin County just north of San Francisco. There are those who claim that the earthquake damage to the Bay area was considerably less than it might have been because of his Holiness's visit just prior to its occurrence.

I had the opportunity to ask his Holiness a question at a press conference held immediately following the Lhasang ceremony. I asked him about the coming together of East and West and what that really means.

THE DALAI LAMA: As I mentioned earlier, these things are a very positive change, a positive development. At a certain stage in a society's development, an authoritarian, very rigid system may work. An example of that might be when the Russian Revolution took place and the Chinese Communist Revolution took place. For a certain period of time, it worked. But I believe that even though this system or ideology had the potential to break through the existing system, it has very little to offer as a new, meaningful way of life. The reason, to me, is quite clear. These revolutionary movements mainly come from hatred, not from love.

Of course, there are advances and a certain kind of love and concern involved. As far as working-class people and less-privileged people are concerned, the advances can seem very good. But compare the hate and energy of power with the energy of love. Compare the force of hatred with the force of compassion. I think the hatred force may be 60, 70, or perhaps 80 percent—and only 20 to 30 percent compassion. Therefore, things cannot work properly. And now we are seeing people who are realizing this situation. People are either compelled to change or compelled to accept things as they are—that's human history, right?

I consider the 20th century one of the most important in human history. Within this century, we've gained many experiences—positive as well as negative. As a result, I think humanity has become more discerning. When things become so dangerous and delicate and fearful, that helps develop human awareness. It took the nuclear attack—so awful, so powerful—to wake up the desire for world peace. After World War II, many people thought a third world war would come inevitably. But because of the nuclear threat, people developed their awareness. So that is hopeful.

The same is true with the environment. We see that it is damaged. The signs of damage are already there. Again, that helped develop human awareness. In the religious field, also, I feel that human awareness is being developed. In the name of different religions, humans have suffered and inflicted great misery. By developing an awareness of other religions, we can open our eyes, our minds, and look with tolerance at the messages of different religions.

❖❖❖

EPILOGUE

The Dalai Lama serves as a model of kindness and compassion for each of us. Here is a man who has lost friends, family, and his nation (more than one million Tibetans have lost their lives since the Chinese takeover in 1959, and this from a nation with less than a population of five million), yet he still exemplifies the ideals he speaks about.

In an emerging global society, the Dalai Lama also addresses the importance of recognizing the sameness inherent in all human beings, whatever their religion, race, or status in society. It's clear that this realization begins at home for each of us. As we're able to practice more kindness and compassion in our daily life, so too will the world change.

❖❖❖ ❖❖❖

CHAPTER TWO

Lovingkindness and Active Peace

Tai Situpa Rinpoche and Michael Toms

PROLOGUE

*F*ollowing a series of groundbreaking visits to Bodhgaya, India; Vatican City, Italy; and Dumfries, Scotland; the 12th Tai Situpa, one of Tibet's most revered lamas, brought his Pilgrimage for Active Peace to San Francisco in October 1989. This far-reaching quest to overcome global conflict and to encourage efforts to promote international understanding began and will end in Bodhgaya, India, site of the Buddha's enlightenment. This unprecedented trek brings together a wide range of the world's religious leaders and several outstanding public figures, including his Holiness the Dalai Lama. By the mid-1990s, more than 100,000 people have participated in events designed to inspire all nations and all cultures to actively pursue environmental, social, and political justice. Tibet is a land where historical leaders are measured by their spiritual attainment, and *biographies are chronicles that span many lifetimes. The Tai Situpas are a line of recognized incarnate monks who are held in the highest esteem by Tibetan Buddhists. Until they were ousted from Tibet for political reasons, the members of the Palpung monastery in eastern Tibet, monastic seat of the Tai Situpas, offered administrative leadership and guidance in spiritual and temporal affairs to more than 13 monastic states and 180 major monastic establishments.*

The current Tai Situpa is the 12th in a line of incarnate Tibetan teachers who have played a vital role in the development and leadership of Tibetan Buddhism since the 14th century. The 12th Tai Situpa is a respected author, teacher, artist, poet, and scholar. Enthroned when he was 18 months old, and exiled from his native Tibet at the age of 6, Tai Situpa Rinpoche, or "Precious One," grew up across the Himalayas in Sikkim. At 22, he assumed his traditional responsibilities by establishing his first monastic project called Sherab Ling, or "Place of Wisdom," at the request of his Tibetan followers who had settled in northern India.

The Tai Situpa's extensive knowledge of traditional Buddhist teaching, combined with his fluency in English and his familiarity with so many Eastern and Western cultures, have given him a valuable perspective on problems such as religious strife, widespread environmental decay, world hunger, and social injustice. In 1982, in response to the growing interest in spirituality in the Western world, the Tai Situpa established Maitreya Institute, a vehicle for intercultural exchange and understanding. Maitreya Institute now has active branches in Honolulu, San Francisco, and Paris.

❖❖❖

MICHAEL TOMS: *Can you tell me when you first had the inspiration and idea to create the Pilgrimage for Active Peace?*

TAI SITUPA RINPOCHE: Actually it was inspired by everything that I have been through—especially the contrasts I have seen—as I traveled both in Eastern and Western countries. As a religious person, I believe religion is a most precious thing, and the essence of religion is very deep and profound. But I also saw what kinds of things can happen in the name of religion. All of these things concerned me, and even in my limited capacity, I felt it was my duty and my responsibility to do whatever I could. So this effort started with personal dedication.

As a Tibetan Buddhist, what do you see that Buddhism and its principles bring to the world relative to peace?

I think that the principle of Buddhism—and the principle of every religion—is related to the reason a great being such as Buddha or Christ or Mohammed taught that religion in the first place. When I look at this subject closely, I see that each founder of a religion taught because he saw that humanity needed guidance. Each of the great religious leaders saw the potential in every person for development and awareness. I think that is the guiding principle of every religion; therefore, in a religion such as Buddhism, the teachings of the Lord Buddha have tremendous potential to impact everyone's future.

As you've been traveling in conjunction with the Pilgrimage for Active Peace, you've been meeting with other religious leaders. What kind of response have you gotten from them?

The Pilgrimage for Active Peace has been active for a little over one month, and the kind of support that I have received within this short time is overwhelming. It is really encouraging. The pilgrimage started in Bodhgaya, where representatives of all

Buddhist orders—Japanese, Sri Lankan, Tibetan, Chinese—participated. From there, we went to Italy, where we had a wonderful intermonastic exchange—not just a dialogue, but a real exchange. All of the participants prayed together at Assisi. After which, in a private audience, his Holiness the Pope read his message of support for the Pilgrimage for Active Peace.

After that, we attended a three-day private meeting with the most eminent individuals—scholars, Nobel laureates, religious representatives, and representatives from the European community. The result was extremely encouraging because all of their ideas overlapped. The meeting resulted in a very good statement and conclusion. The event in San Francisco followed, and the forthcoming event in Mt. Shasta will happen a few days from now.

These have all been a tremendous inspiration to me. Everyone's enthusiasm is amazing. And his Holiness the Dalai Lama accepted the invitation for the Pilgrimage for Active Peace here at the San Francisco event, as well as for a New Delhi event. His presence here offered great encouragement. I feel this is going in the right direction and that there is a tremendous potential yet to be realized.

A few days ago, his Holiness was awarded the Nobel Prize for Peace. How do you see this affecting not only the Pilgrimage but the world at large?

I think this will make a tremendous impact. It doesn't change his Holiness the Dalai Lama; whether he has the Nobel Peace Prize or not, he is the same person. But because of the world recognition he receives by winning the Nobel Peace Prize, more people will be interested in learning what he is all about. In that way, I think it will be a tremendous benefit. I also think that this is a great encouragement to all the people who are working so hard trying to improve the conditions of life around us. It is encouraging that the Nobel committee recognizes that kind of effort.

You mention the Mt. Tamalpais event as part of the Pilgrimage for Active Peace where his Holiness appeared along with you, and you did a traditional Tibetan Lhasang ceremony to heal the environment. In the news conference afterwards, in response to a question, his Holiness mentioned that he wanted to see education change so that there was education for encouraging the good heart. How do you see that, and what do you see as "the good heart"?

What I understood was that "good heart" means compassion. I thought that's what his Holiness meant. I believe that if a majority of people develop compassion, this world will definitely be a different place. Developing compassion—a good heart—is, in my view, a necessary and positive action.

His Holiness also expressed an optimism and a hopefulness about the future. Do you have the same optimism?

I experience different situations in different ways. Sometimes good things happen without much work. Sometimes good things happen only after tremendous, extraordinary work. And sometimes, even if you work very hard, things go wrong. Some situations make me feel optimistic, but some situations make me feel a little bit discouraged because certain things go wrong or get misunderstood unnecessarily. But one thing that does give me a sense of optimism, despite everything else, is that no matter what is going on here right now, deep inside every person is the potential to be loved and to be loving and to have compassion. So that definitely makes me feel hopeful.

Perhaps you could describe the ceremony that you and his Holiness the Dalai Lama were conducting on the mountain as a healing of the environment. What is the purpose of it?

Lhasang is a traditional Tibetan Buddhist ceremony. The purpose of this ceremony is to create a harmonious balance between the spirits of the area—the mountain, the river, the lake, the air, the space—and the people who live there. Harmony is necessary because people dominate the area and do whatever they like.

The land gets abused. The environment gets abused. This ceremony was specifically for the Mt. Tamalpais prayer session, and it was meant to help people realize the consequences of their ignorance. Most of the time, people aren't destroying the environment knowingly, but out of ignorance.

Is the purpose of the Pilgrimage for Active Peace "environmental peace-keeping" as much as it is political peace-keeping?

Each time we meet, we discuss all the things—not just war—that will destroy life on Earth. Definitely war and weapons have to be overcome, and we should work very hard to have a world without war. But we also need to consider what is happening in the environment and the global economy.

To know the effect pollution has on living conditions, we have to consider a variety of factors, including how much the desert is expanding every day, how many kilometers of ocean are being polluted every day, changes in the weather, and destruction of the ozone layer. If pollution continues at its current rate, 50 years from now it may be too late to repair the damage. It will be very much like a world where a major war has taken place. According to a United Nations report, all over the world, especially in Third World countries, 40,000 children die every day due to lack of food, poor hygiene, inadequate medicine and medical facilities, and a deteriorating environment. At the same time, these countries spend enormous amounts of money on their weapons.

We call our project "active peace" for a very specific reason. To improve quality of life worldwide, we all have to work actively and constantly to make peace—not only among nations, but between humanity and the environment.

Does praying for peace help?

Prayer does a lot because it comes from the heart. If you pray sincerely, it will definitely have an impact—not only on you, but on your neighbors, friends, and everyone else. But prayer alone is not enough. Because of the speed at which we seem to be going in the wrong direction right now, we need to combine prayer with action.

Tibet has been under Chinese martial law for several years, particularly Lhasa and regions around Lhasa. How do you see that situation changing?

I think it will take a very deep kind of political involvement on everyone's part—the Tibetans, the Chinese, everyone. Therefore, overcoming all the difficulties will take time. But I am always hopeful. Because with our combined efforts, everything will be better—not only for Tibetans, not only for Chinese, but for everyone in this world. Every situation will improve.

❖❖❖

EPILOGUE

Tai Situpa Rinpoche carries on the theme begun by the Dalai Lama, the development of "the good heart," through fostering compassion. It's important to note that the Buddhist view of compassion is an active one. Compassion is not seen as a passive, detached-from-the-dailyness-of-the-world activity, but rather is an engaged and passionate commitment to bring this ethic into all aspects of life. Situpa Rinpoche is advocating what is known as "engaged Buddhism," which you will read more about within these pages. Spirituality, as seen from the Buddhist perspective, is both an inner and outer process. If your spiritual practice does not help you in the everyday world of activity, then of what benefit is it?

❖❖❖ ❖❖❖

CHAPTER THREE

The Essence of Buddhist Wisdom

Thich Nhat Hanh and Michael Toms

PROLOGUE

*"The other may be a beautiful sunrise. The other
may be your friend, your husband, your wife. The other is
love. Mindfulness helps you recognize what is there that
makes life real, that makes life possible."*
— Thich Nhat Hanh, on the art of mindfulness

❖❖❖

*B*uddhist monk Thich Nhat Hanh is one of the world's most
admired religious leaders. Born in Vietnam in 1926, and a
monk since the age of 16, Thich Nhat Hanh first achieved international notoriety in 1966 when he was exiled from his native Vietnam
for his efforts to end the Vietnam war. That same year, Thich Nhat
Hanh came to the United States "to describe to Americans the aspi-

rations and the agony of the voiceless masses of the Vietnamese people." He also met with influential leaders, including Secretary of Defense Robert MacNamara, Senator Edward Kennedy, Thomas Merton, and Martin Luther King, Jr., who nominated Thich Nhat Hanh for the Nobel Peace Prize the following year. Since then, Thich Nhat Hanh has continued to work as an advocate for peace, aiding war refugees and uniting people of all nationalities, races, religions, and sexes to expose them to "mindfulness." This is the Zen practice of embracing the present, being profoundly aware of each moment so that people can better appreciate their own lives, and being more compassionate about the suffering of others.

Thich Nhat Hanh visits the United States every other year to speak to crowds that number in the thousands and to lead interfaith retreats on the art of mindful living. His teachings appeal to a wide audience, drawing Christians, Jews, atheists, and Zen followers alike. Thich Nhat Hanh is the author of Living Buddha, Living Christ.

❖❖❖

MICHAEL TOMS: *What do you see as the parallels or differences between the Christian trinity—the Father, Son, and Holy Spirit—and the three Buddhist jewels—Buddha, Dharma, and Sangha?*

THICH NHAT HANH: The holy spirit is the energy of God. You gain access to God if you get in touch with the Holy Spirit. The same thing is true in Buddhism. If you have access to mindfulness, you embody the life of a Sangha because a Sangha is a community that lives in mindfulness. And mindfulness allows you to touch the Dharma, to make the Dharma alive, and it also allows you to touch the Buddha. If you approach God the Father, you might have difficulty with your ideas, your notions concerning God, and that is why touching the Holy Spirit, the energy of God, which is equivalent to mindfulness in Buddhism, would be an easier way to touch God. Wherever there is understanding, there is acceptance, there is love, and that is the Holy Spirit. Christians and non-Christians are able to recognize that presence. Therefore, to practice in such a way that the Holy Spirit can be present is the best way to offer God to people around you, and, of course, to offer God to yourself. A Sangha that is alive always contains the Dharma and the Buddha. A community that has the spirit of God, that has the energy of the Holy Spirit, can always offer God the Father and God the Son to its members and to the world.

Many Christians don't believe that Buddhists believe in God. What is your response to that?

If you describe God as the Ground of Being, then it is quite easy to accept God as the Ground of Being, the Ultimate Dimension of reality. There is a fruit called a *banana* in English. In Asia, they call that fruit by another name. The Vietnamese would call it *Dtuie*. The French, *banane*. But they all point to the same object. What is important, then, is the essence of an entity, and we should not be caught up in words or notions. We have to penetrate the reality. Christians say that God is love, which is easy for Buddhists to understand. Buddhists say that if you don't understand, you can never love. Love and understanding must be the same thing. If you cannot understand, you cannot love. Therefore, when you say God is love, you have to say at the same time that love is understanding. Understanding is enlightenment. And enlightenment is the essence of the Buddha.

Buddhists not only believe, but they know, that within each of us there is a seat of understanding, a seat of love, a seat of enlightenment. And if you doubt the existence of these seats, you doubt

❖ 21

the Buddha, you doubt the Dharma, and you doubt the Sangha. The same thing is true in Christianity. You say that God is in your heart. God is love. And if you don't believe that you have the capacity of understanding, of loving, you doubt God. We have to make an effort to understand the language of others. Then we can remove our wrong notions about other traditions, and that is the practice of understanding, the practice of peace, the practice of reconciliation that each tradition would like to follow.

There is the idea of "soul" in Christianity. How would you define soul? Is there a soul in Buddhism?

Buddhists talk about body and mind—name and form. In this case, *name* means the psychological factors, and *form* means the body. The human body is made of five factors: form, which is the body; then feelings; perceptions; mental formations; and consciousness. Looking deeply into these five elements, you don't see anything permanent. You acknowledge the presence of feelings, perceptions, other mental formations, and your consciousness, but you don't see any permanent entity that underlies all of these elements. Therefore, if you understand soul as the presence of feelings, mental formations, perceptions, and consciousness, then the Buddhist can say that the soul exists. But if you say that the soul is something that remains the same forever, something that never changes, something that exists without a body, the Buddhist cannot see that. Because the body, according to the teaching of the Buddha, is one of the conditions that makes the feelings, perceptions, and mental formations manifest.

The teaching of impermanence is fundamental in Buddhism. Everything is impermanent. Not only your body is impermanent, but your feelings, your perceptions, your mental formations, and your consciousness. Believing in something permanent is not only *not* Buddhist, it's not scientific. The teaching of impermanence should not be seen as negative or pessimistic. It is thanks to impermanence that everything is here. If a grain of corn, for example, were not impermanent, it could never become a corn plant, and we'd never have more corn to eat. If there were no impermanence, illness could never be cured. Instead of complaining that things are impermanent, we must welcome impermanence as a factor that makes life possible.

If you practice looking deeply into the nature of things, into the nature of impermanence, you will see that nothing has a separate existence. A flower, for example, cannot have a separate existence because a flower relies on "nonflower" elements in order to exist. If you look at a flower, you see a cloud, because if the cloud is not there, there will be no rain. You look into the flower, and you see the sunshine. If the rain and the sunshine were not there, the flower could not grow. You can also see the gardener, the earth—many things. So we can say that a flower is made only of nonflower elements, and that is what we call "nonself." Nonself means the absence of a separate existence. You and I and the flower are without a separate self. We rely on each other in order to exist.

Impermanence and nonself are the insights that come when we observe things deeply. If what is called the soul is something that is permanent, that remains the same thing forever, then that notion of the soul cannot be accepted because it is impossible for Buddhists to find something that remains the same forever and ever—something that can have a separate existence and not rely on anything else in order to exist. But the truth of impermanence, the truth of nonself, must not be called a Buddhist truth, because it has a universal value. Whether you are a Buddhist or a non-Buddhist, you have to accept the nature of impermanence and of nonself. So the notion of soul has to be observed in such a way that it can reveal its nature to us. Otherwise, it would be caught in an idea that has nothing to do with reality as it is.

You mentioned nonself, and you've written about the island of the self and cultivating the mind of heart. Can you describe what you mean by that?

In order to communicate, one needs words. As far as we are aware that a self is made only of nonself elements, it is safe for us to use the word *self* and to use the notion of self. But if we think of self as something that can be by itself—alone—such a thing does not exist. In that context, it could be dangerous to use the word *self* and the notion of self. We can talk about self, provided we know that self is always made of nonself elements.

Many of the people who come to your retreats and read your books are Christians, Jews—Westerners. In your book Living Buddha, Living Christ, *you wrote that it was important to cultivate one's root tradition, one's cultural tradition, and one's religious tradition. How do you see the future? Do you see something such as Christian Buddhists or Buddhist Christians?*

I have seen and met people who practice Buddhism and Christianity at the same time, and they see no conflict in themselves. There are Catholic priests who have come to me and asked for the three refuges and the five precepts and are very happy to receive them. They don't see any conflict between their belief in God and the idea of the three refuges and the five precepts. They are very Buddhist in their nature, which means they are very open-minded. They accept anything that is true, that is good, and that is beautiful. God is something true, something good, and something beautiful. And when people are not caught by ideas and words, it is wonderful. I have met such people, and I think they are our future.

We must not be divided by the fringes of ideology and religion. Christianity is a spiritual heritage of humankind. Buddhism is also part of that heritage. As human beings, we have the right to profit from those and other spiritual traditions. If you like oranges, you are welcome to continue eating oranges, but it would be a pity if you refused to eat other kinds of fruit. The same thing is true with our spiritual heritages. You can be a Buddhist. You can enjoy the values, the jewels of your tradition, but you have to open yourself to receive the beauty—the jewels—of other traditions such as Christianity, Judaism, and so on.

In Korea, where I visited this spring, we attended a conference that presented a dialogue between Buddhists and Christians. I proposed that we let the people of the two traditions marry freely. In Asia, a young man and woman of the two traditions are not allowed to marry freely. I said that when people of the two traditions get married, they have an opportunity to study and practice the spiritual tradition of the other person. Not only do they *not* have to abandon their roots, but they will grow other roots and become stronger. When they give birth to their children, they will encourage their children to embrace both traditions. For example, the husband might tell his wife, "The next full-moon day when you go to the Buddhist temple, I will go with you to offer flowers to the Buddha." The wife will say, "My husband, next Sunday when you go to church, I will go with you, and I will participate in the Eucharist with you." That would be wonderful. That would be our future, because if people of different religious traditions can live with each other in that way, we can avoid war and conflict. People will be much happier in that spirit of openness.

There are critics—including the present Pope—who would say that one risks the danger of losing one's present faith if one embraces another religion. What about that criticism?

I think that kind of feeling has fear at its root. In fact, if we are concerned only with the form of practice, we have already lost the essence of religion. It is exactly the dialogue with other traditions that can help us recover the essence of the tradition that we have lost. First, we have to establish a dialogue with the people in our own tradition. Buddhism, for example, consists of Tibetan Buddhism, Japanese Buddhism, Korean Buddhism, Vietnamese Buddhism, Chinese Buddhism, Theravada Buddhism, and Mahayana Buddhism. These groups all belong to the tradition of Buddhism, but when they get together, practice together, and learn from each other, they can restore what they have lost in their own tradition. Not only do we lose ourselves, but we recover ourselves and we enrich ourselves, which is very important. In Christianity, the Orthodox church, the Protestant church, and the Catholic church can do the same thing. If the three traditions come together and establish a genuine dialogue, they can recover a lot of things that each of them may have lost.

After starting the dialogue within our own religious families, we can then open the dialogue to other religious traditions. We can gain a lot of insight, and not only can we recover what we have lost, but we can enrich ourselves and offer the best that we have to other traditions. That is why fear is not justified. Dialogue is always a wonderful path for growth. It helps us to be reborn, to renew ourselves, and to be vigorous again.

In Living Buddha, Living Christ, *you wrote, "I try to practice in a way that allows me to touch my blood ancestors and my spiritual ancestors every day." What do you mean by that?*

Our ancestors are always with us. But if we feel too separate from our ancestors, have problems with our ancestors, or feel angry with our ancestors, we need to practice connecting with them. We are a continuation of our ancestors, and we cannot say that we have nothing to do with them. When we practice looking deeply into ourselves, we see that we *are* our ancestors. We are the continuation of our ancestors, so it is very important to accept them. When we employ the Buddhist practice of "touching the earth," we surrender our so-called self in order to connect with our ancestors—to enter into the stream of our ancestors. If we can do that, we can establish the root circulation again in our stream of life. That will help us recover our health, our joy, and our communication—not only with our ancestors, but also with our progeny.

To feel connected with our blood ancestors and our spiritual ancestors is very important. We get a lot of strength when we feel connected with our ancestors, and we can transmit a lot of strength to our children and grandchildren, but our spiritual ancestors are also very real in us. Spiritual ancestors have nourished us; they have transmitted to us the capacity to understand, to love, to accept, to be joyful and alive. Maybe because of our feelings of loneliness or feelings of being cut off from our ancestors, we cannot touch the seats of joy, peace, and love that are buried in us. They have been transmitted to us by our ancestors, and when we practice connecting with our ancestors, we water these beautiful seeds and suddenly communication, love, and acceptance become possible again. They bring joy and happiness. They will make our children and our grandchildren happy. The practice of connecting with our ancestors is very important, and we all have to practice no matter whether we are Buddhist or non-Buddhist, Christian or non-Christian, Jewish or non-Jewish.

You've written about the importance of having a Sangha to practice with. What does that mean?

A Sangha is a community, such as a church, in which brothers and sisters practice together. The presence of these brothers and sisters serves to support and nourish each other. If you practice alone, you may abandon your practice in a few months. Everyone needs a Sangha because only a Sangha can carry, in a powerful way, the presence of the Buddha, of the Dharma. "Wherever three or four of you gather in my name, I'll be there," Jesus said. Everyone needs a Sangha to continue his or her practice. In my tradition, we say, "If a tiger leaves his mountain and goes to the lowland, he will be caught by humans and killed." A practitioner leaving his or her community of practice will abandon his or her practice very soon.

If your Sangha, your community, is not strong enough, it means that the Holy Spirit is not very strong, and you have to practice in a way to make the Holy Spirit present and stronger. If your Buddhist Sangha does not have enough energy of mindfulness, loving, and understanding, then you have to practice in a way to bring in more of those things. Don't give up. If you practice correctly, you will be like a torch, and you will enlighten the other brothers and sister in your community. Together you will make the energy of mindfulness present in your community. If mindfulness is there, then the Dharma and the Buddha are also there.

In the Christian community, the Holy Spirit should be there as the substance of the church. If you don't feel the presence of the Holy Ghost in your church, then try to practice as a good Christian. Influence your church by your presence, by your good practice, and then together with other brothers and sisters in the church, you will help bring back the Holy Spirit. When the Holy Spirit is alive there, God the Son is there, God the Father is there. Everyone will profit from such a church, such a community of practice.

In Buddhism, we say, "I take refuge in my Sangha," which means that we take refuge in our spiritual community. The same is true in Christianity. We all need a church, a community of practice, to go on and succeed in our practice. It is important that people build up a Sangha, build up a group of friends, so that they might support each other in their practice. We have been helping friends set up Sanghas everywhere and helping them practice mindfulness in more than 20 countries. These are now places where people can nourish and support each other in their practice.

You are called the "Father of Engaged Buddhism," and you take your practice of mindfulness into the world in a socially relevant way. In the United States, there's a great deal of confusion about engaged Buddhism, mindfulness, and the relationship to one's practice, one's spiritual path. How do Westerners incorporate these concepts into their lives?

Mindfulness is the kind of energy that helps us live deeply each moment of our daily life. When I drink water, I try to drink it mindfully. I drink my water in such a way that I become real, and the water becomes real. At the moment I drink my water, life is there. Mindfulness is there. The opposite of mindfulness is forgetfulness. Forgetfulness is not there. When you are there, I try to be there with you. I am mindful of your presence, so I am real, you are real, and that moment is true life. Mindfulness makes life true and real. When we touch ourselves with mindfulness, *we* become real and true. When we touch the world with mindfulness, *the world* becomes true and real. With mindfulness, we reveal things in all their beauty, their meaning. That is why we speak of mindfulness as the substance of the Buddha.

With mindfulness, we acknowledge the presence of the other. The other may be the full moon. The other may be the cherry blossom. The other may be a beautiful sunrise. The other may be a friend, a husband, or a wife. The other is love. Mindfulness helps us recognize what is there. It makes life real. It makes life possible. And mindfulness is practiced not only in temples and monasteries. Mindfulness should be practiced in our daily life. When we drive, we drive mindfully. When we go shopping, we shop mindfully. If we do things mindfully, we avoid making mistakes so that we will not create suffering for ourselves and the world. For example, if we drink alcohol, but we drink it mindfully, we'll be able to see that drinking alcohol is harmful to ourselves and to the world. We spend so much energy and grain to make alcohol, yet we deprive many people in the world of food. By drinking alcohol mindfully, we can recognize the fact that it is not a very friendly act toward people who are starving. Drinking alcohol mindfully helps us to become enlightened, and it helps us stop drinking alcohol.

If we are doing something such as protecting the environment, if we are able to avoid using materials that can pollute our ecosystem, and if we do it mindfully, then we will be nourished by our joy and hope, because we know that we are living our real life in such a way that a future will be possible for our children and our grandchildren. That joy will nourish us and make us happy. That is mindfulness.

Mindfulness is the energy that is so needed at this time in history. Mindfulness will help us stop doing the things that continue to destroy our world, things that cause misery and suffering in our society. Mindfulness helps us to understand the situation, helps us to love in such a way that we can relieve suffering and bring joy and happiness to ourselves and the people around us. That is why the practice of mindfulness is not the business of monks or nuns alone. Practicing mindfulness is everyone's business.

Mindfulness is the ability to know what is going on in the present moment. Not knowing what is going on can be dangerous. A journalist, for example, practices mindfulness in order to be aware of what is going on, and he or she practices mindfulness to help other people be aware of what is going on. This is very important. An educator also has to practice mindfulness in order to know how to educate others. We all need to be educated. We all need to know about the world situation. To educate also means to help us become aware of our true needs and of the dangers that are waiting for us. In this way, we can avoid the dangers, and we can orient ourselves in the direction of our needs. An educator should tell us what is the right thing to consume and what is not the right thing to consume. If we don't consume properly, we destroy our bodies, we destroy our consciousness, and we destroy the world. The politician must also practice mindfulness to know what is going on in society, in the minds of people. Mindfulness helps the politician respond to his or her true needs and the needs of the people. If mindfulness is not there, the politician will only serve his or her ego and interests, and not really work for us and our well-being. Whatever our station in life, we all have to practice mindfulness.

You've also written about the idea of compassionate listening, the ability to listen deeply. Can you expand on that?

When we are mindful, we notice that another person suffers. The other person may be a husband, a wife, or a child. If one person suffers, that person needs to talk to someone in order to get relief. We have to offer our presence, and we have to listen deeply to the person who is suffering. That is the practice of love—deep listening. But if we are full of anger, irritation, and prejudices, we don't have the capacity to listen deeply to the people we love. If people we love cannot communicate with us, then they will suffer more. Learning how to listen deeply is our responsibility. We are motivated by the desire to relieve suffering. That is why we listen. We need to listen with all our heart, without intention to judge, condemn, or criticize. And if we listen in that way for one hour, we are practicing true love. We don't have to say anything; we just need to listen.

These days, we have many sophisticated ways to communicate—faxes, e-mail, telephones, and televisions. But many people have lost the capacity to communicate on a personal level. The practice of mindful listening, of mindful speaking, of compassionate listening, is crucial to restoring harmony, peace, and understanding to the family and to society. If we are capable of restoring communication between family members, between factions of a nation, then we can restore harmony and understanding. If we are able to do that, we will be able to restore communication between countries that are in conflict. We know that guns and bombs cannot solve these conflicts, and that is why the practice of listening deeply needs to be implemented on the level of international affairs. But if we cannot succeed in doing it in our families, in our own nations, how can we do it on the international level? That is why mindful listening, compassionate listening, and mindful speech, are very important practices in our daily life.

❖❖❖

EPILOGUE

Growing and acting from one's spiritual center in today's world is an enormous challenge and cannot be done without help. With Olympian levels of distraction surrounding us, it's necessary now more than ever to cultivate spiritual friends and include them as an integral part of our daily lives. Thich Nhat Hanh speaks of the need for spiritual community to support one's growth and practice. In Buddhism, this kind of community is called a sangha.

Additionally, he details the reasons why understanding the nonself, mindfulness, and impermanence are qualities necessary for life in a challenging world. The importance of dialogue with others, particularly those of other traditions and maintaining our connection to both our blood and spiritual ancestors, is also emphasized by Thich Nhat Hanh. Perhaps most important are his remarks about the practice of mindfulness and learning to listen deeply. It begins within our own families, communities, and nations.

❖❖❖ ❖❖❖

CHAPTER FOUR

Buddhism: Past, Present, and Future

Stephen Batchelor
and Michael Toms

PROLOGUE

*B*uddhism *is said to be the fastest-growing religion and one of the most influential spiritual movements in North America and Europe. It has become clear that Buddhism is playing a significant role in the new planetary culture and one quite different from the usual East–West encounters of the past. Even though Western civilization has been aware of Buddhism for 2,000 years, it is only within the very recent past that the West has emerged from its previous cultural arrogance with respect to this remarkably practical spiritual path. Therein lies a fascinating story, and it forms the focus of the following discussion with Stephen Batchelor.*

Stephen Batchelor was born in Scotland and educated in Buddhist monasteries in India, Korea, and Switzerland. He's a renowned Buddhist teacher and scholar, the author of A Guide to the Bodhisattva's Way of Life, The Faith to Doubt, Alone with

Others, An Existential Approach to Buddhism, The Tibet Guide, The Awakening of the West: Encounter of Buddhism in Western Culture, *and* Buddhism Without Beliefs.

❖❖❖

MICHAEL TOMS: *When did you first become exposed to Buddhism?*

STEPHEN BATCHELOR: This occurred for me in the early 1970s. I left high school at the age of 18, and instead of going into the university, I chose to travel overland to India. It took me six months or so, and I ended up in Dharmsala, where the Dalai Lama was exiled. I studied there for three years, during which time I became a Tibetan Buddhist monk. After that I went to Switzerland to another monastery with my teacher who had been appointed abbot there. I studied primarily philosophy, psychology, epistemology, and logic for another four years. After that I chose to focus my practice more on direct meditational experience, and this took me to South Korea, where I trained for four years in a Zen monastery. After that I returned to England, where I married, and I now live in a nondenominational Buddhist community.

Did you go to India with the intention of becoming a monk?

When I left England, I had no intention of even going to India. It was somewhat in the atmosphere at that time—travel meant, ultimately, going east. I sort of drifted out there really. When I arrived in Dharmsala, it was almost by chance that I stumbled upon an institute that had just opened. It was offering courses in Buddhism to Westerners. I enrolled and just stayed there, and in a sense my life changed at that point. Instead of traveling the outer surface of the world, I moved the journey inward to explore the realms of mind, spirit, and so on. I hadn't intended to become a monk; I hadn't really thought of these things. But as I became more absorbed in my studies, as I took them more seriously, that became the logical thing to do. Becoming a monk would enable me to have a lifestyle that would be entirely dedicated to the practices and studies that I most wished to do.

After spending seven years with the Tibetans in a few different monasteries, what led you to Korea?

It's a fairly complex story. I was training in the Gelug tradition of Tibetan Buddhism, which emphasizes a firm, scholarly understanding of Buddhist philosophy. This is a good underpinning in what Buddhism is actually about. So I learned the Tibetan language, both the spoken and classical. I studied many texts, and I found this extremely enriching. But I did feel that there was perhaps too much of an emphasis on the scholarly aspect, and I wanted to correct the imbalance. So I began to concentrate on a more focused meditational training. I did initially consider going into a lengthy three-year retreat under Tibetan guidance, but I found that those kind of retreats also seemed somewhat complex in the details of mandalas and so on that one had to familiarize oneself with.

For many years, I'd been drawn to the directness and the paradoxes and the kind of earthiness of Zen Buddhism. This led me to seek a teacher in that tradition. I chose Korea because the monastic tradition, as in Tibetan Buddhism, was still preserved. I could live as a monk. I could undergo a training that was far more intense than it would have been had I gone to Japan. We sat in meditation for three months at a time, twice a year. We were focusing on a very simple question: "What is this?" That was it, and I loved it.

How would you contrast your experience with Zen and your experience with Tibetan Buddhism? How would you describe the differences to someone who had never heard of Buddhism or just was learning about Buddhism?

Tibetan Buddhism has the great strength of being extremely comprehensive. It's probably the only Buddhist school that really retains the full complexity of a living Buddhist culture. It is extraordinarily rich, its study encompassing the reflections, the meditations, the philosophy, and the psychology, whereas in Zen you have a very single-pointed focus on a very basic question. There is no philosophy, no psychology, no epistemology. I would try to discuss these issues with my Zen teacher. I'd try to argue with him. He'd follow to a point, and then he would say, "But do you really understand? Do you really know?" And I would find myself unable to say anything. Then go back and sit. After a while, I realized that was all I was really there to do—simply focus on the basic questions. But what I found, unexpectedly perhaps, was that the pared-down meditative practice helped me appreciate the depths of the studies that I'd been doing with the Tibetans. I also found that the two went together extremely well. Zen Buddhism provided me with a kind of vertical dimension that added depth to the horizontal richness of Tibetan Buddhism. I don't see them at all in contrast or conflict. I find that they merge and support each other extremely well.

After 11 years in the monastery, what prompted you to leave and pursue a different kind of life?

A number of things led to my decision. My Zen teacher died, and with his death the Zen monastery underwent a great change. He didn't really have a successor. Also, I had completed the period of training to which I had committed myself when I first arrived. When I'd left Europe four years before, I had already felt that I didn't want to play the role of a Buddhist monk in a European context. I felt that the sheer presence of a monastic robe and a shaved head tended to create a barrier between me and others. People related to me as a representative of an institution rather than as another human being. So I already had severe doubts about living in the West as a monk. The third factor, perhaps the crucial one, was that I fell in love with my wife. She was also living in Korea. She was a nun and had been training in Zen Buddhism for about ten years. We decided that we would return together. So we disrobed. And then we settled in this community in Britain.

Most of us are not aware that Westerners were exposed to Buddhism about 2,000 years ago. Alexander the Great came in contact with Buddhism, and so did some of his successors. Maybe you could discuss how far back the contact goes.

There is, in fact, a mention of the West in early Buddhist scriptures, where the Buddha uses the example of the Greeks in India to make a point about the caste system. But it seems unlikely that the Buddha had actually encountered Greeks, because the Greek communities were a long way from where he was teaching. It doesn't seem that Alexander the Great would have actually met Buddhist monks. In all likelihood, he met what we would call Sadhus today, wandering ascetics. Perhaps they were Jains, but almost certainly not Buddhists.

It wasn't until the subsequent Greek invasions of Menander, about 300 years later, that there was an encounter between Greek rulers and citizens living in India in colonies who became absorbed into the Buddhist culture of northwest India. That was quite a profound process of assimilation. It affected the Indian Buddhists, in a sense, in a longer-term way than it did the Greeks. The image of the Buddha, for example, was a creation of the Greeks. Until the Greek communities came along, there was no representation of the Buddha in a human form. Their representation was based on the image of Apollo. This is a remarkable fact, because the image of the Buddha as a human being has been vital to the spread of Buddhism and to our awareness of it.

It is also strange that the Greeks in India who knew about Buddhism did not take that knowledge back to Greece itself. Outside of India, the Greeks remained quite ignorant of Buddhism and anything it meant. The Neoplatonists had a vague sense of Indian philosophy in general, but never to the point where they were able to distinguish between the different currents within those traditions.

After the Greek colonists in India, the next encounter was not until the 13th century, when the first Christian friars went out to negotiate with the Mongol Khans, who at that time had expanded through Asia, the Middle East, Russia, and Eastern Europe. These first contacts were about 1,700 years after the time of the Buddha. At that time, Christianity in Europe had expanded into a very rich and very mature tradition. Similarly, Buddhism in Asia had expanded throughout China and Japan by that period. And yet the two cultures had grown up in basic ignorance of one another, which is surprising from our point of view now—but the world was a larger place then.

Were there Buddhist traders traveling through the holy land around the time of Christ? There are so many parallels in the Gnostic tradition to Buddhism that it seems almost certain that there was some exchange of information going on.

There certainly was an exchange of information. You find, for example, in the fables of Aesop, stories that you also find in the Buddhist *Jataka,* or birth tales. It seems likely that the story of Christ told in the Gospels was modeled to some extent on the story of the Buddha. This folk culture existed between Asia and Europe that was conveyed by the trade routes, by the merchants. Stories were exchanged. The difficulty is to know who started them first. Probably both sources influenced each other, and at that level, certainly, there was a sort of common culture emerging.

The Gnostics were aware of the Buddha; and Mani, the founder of Manichaeanism, saw himself as the fulfillment of the prophetic tradition. Zoroaster, Christ, Mani, and very probably many of the other Gnostic teachers were influenced by Indian ideas, but only one of them, Basilides, who's not such a well-known Gnostic, was probably influenced by a specific form of Buddhism. So there were crosscurrents, but never to the point where there was a clear understanding, either in Asia of the eastern Mediterranean traditions, or in Europe of the Buddhist or Hindu traditions.

The reason the Westerners made contact with the Mongols around the 13th century was basically to convert them, wasn't it?

That was the entire idea. The Mongols were a tribal people who burst out of the steppes. They were not a cultured people at all, and they dominated these very civilized areas of the world and sought to draw from those cultures. The Chinese, the Tibetans, the Persians, and the Christians were all knocking on the Khan's door saying, "We've got the truth. Listen to us. Become a Muslim, become a Christian, become a Buddhist." The Khan, in the middle of the 13th century, set up a debate between these conflicting religious groups, and it really was the first time in which such a diversity of religious opinion was put on a similar platform. All views were discussed, but in the end, the Mongols opted for Buddhism. At least the Mongols in China did. Kublai Khan became a Tibetan Buddhist. Christianity never really took off. The Mongols felt it was too exclusive. The friars, in particular, William of Rubrude, from whom we have the best record of the time, was actually evicted by the Mongols for being intolerant.

In the next phase, after that of the 13th century, we have the Jesuits, highly intelligent men of the Renaissance, but fanatical Christians. They sought to convert the heathen Buddhists, Muslims, Hindus, and everyone else to what was to them the truth. For that reason, it was not possible for them to enter into a dialogue. Theirs was the true way; everyone else was in error. Buddhism was perceived as a creation of the devil, which led to hostile encounters. The Buddhists often welcomed Christian missionaries into their temples and monasteries, but quickly discovered there was no reciprocal friendship offered by the Jesuits. In fact, the Europeans perceived the Buddhists as inferior specimens. It was really very sad, but symptomatic of those times. And the Jesuits, of course, were linked in with the whole expansion of European colonialism. They were the vanguard of the West's attempt to dominate the East, and in a sense, they succeeded. Not in the short term, of course, but in the long term, the West has managed to project its philosophical, religious, and political beliefs pretty much throughout the world. And we witness the fruits of it today.

What I find interesting in studying the history of Buddhism and the West is to examine Western history in the broadest strokes. That allows one to see how so much of what we experience today is the result of many hundreds of years of interaction, hostility, and struggle. And we bear the fruits. The irony, of course, is that while the West has dominated the world economically, and to some extent politically, that very dominance has been accompanied by a breakdown in its own spiritual, religious sense. It has lost its sense of purpose, direction, and meaning; while Buddhism, Hinduism, and Taoism are penetrating the West in very calm, peaceful, and unobtrusive ways. A further irony is that the religions of the East are working toward healing the crisis the West has brought upon itself.

You indicated that Kublai Khan became a Tibetan Buddhist. The connection between the Mongolians and the Tibetans still continues to this day, doesn't it?

There is certainly a connection between the two. After converting to Tibetan Buddhism, Mongolia became a Buddhist state very much along the lines of Tibet. They had the grand Hutuktu Lama in Urga, which is now Ulan Bator. He ruled much as the Dalai Lama ruled in Tibet. Now that Mongolia has broken away from the influence of the former Soviet Union, the Mongolian Buddhist tradition is making a strong resurgence.

There are also Mongolian Buddhist communities in Russia, in the Russian Federation in Buriatia, that are also reviving now. In fact, the very first Buddhist temple in Europe was in St. Petersburg, and it was a Mongol Buriat, a Tibetan Buddhist temple. There has been a great Buddhist influence throughout the East. Had there not been the communist takeover in 1917, it's very possible the West would have encountered Buddhism coming through Russia. The Russian Revolution, of course, stopped its spread.

Weren't there also some Chinese and Tibetan partnerships over the centuries?

Periodically, there were Chinese emperors who were very devoted to Tibetan lamas. In the Imperial Court in China through the Ming and Manchu periods, Tibetan lamas were employed often as magicians of a sort. They would recite prayers and do rituals in order to preserve the harmony of the Chinese state. Some of the emperors certainly seemed to have a personal commitment to the teachings of Tibetan Buddhism, but this fluctuated with each dynasty.

Didn't the Tai Situ and the Situpa lineage have a connection with the Chinese?

Tai is, of course, the Chinese word for "great." It is a Chinese title. In the Ming period, in particular, during the 14th and 15th centuries, many Tibetan lamas were invited to China by the emperor, and they were given grandiose titles—the Karmapa, the Tai Situpa. Tsong Khapa of the Gelug was also invited. There was quite a traffic between the two cultures.

As a historian and a scholar, how would you respond to China's assertion that Tibet has always been a part of China?

It is a spurious claim. The periods in which China had the most influence over Tibet were during the Yuan period, or the Mongol period, and most recently during the Manchu period. The Yuan period was in the 13th century—the time of Kublai Khan. The Manchu period lasted from the beginning of the 18th century until the beginning of the 20th century. What's interesting is that neither of those dynasties were Chinese dynasties. They were dynasties ruled by Mongolians and Manchurians who took over the Chinese empire. At that time, there were certainly very strong links, but to call Tibet a part of China on that basis is an extremely spurious claim.

Nevertheless—and this is what's troubling—in China today, the vast majority of the Chinese people do believe that Tibet is the backyard of China. They think of the Tibetans as a rather unruly group of Chinese. Historical arguments notwithstanding, the fact remains that the Chinese perceive Tibet in that way. And it's not just the communists or the nationalists—even most of the student leaders in Tiananmen Square believed Tibet to be part of China. That is the real problem, because the Chinese don't actually see it as a subject that is open for discussion. They are so deeply immured in that perception.

It has only been within the last 20 or 30 years that Buddhism has really taken off in the West, isn't that right?

The practice of Buddhism by Westerners only started at the beginning of this century, and there was a very gradual increase in interest throughout the first 50 years of this century. It was only in the '50s and '60s that it exploded exponentially. And in the last 20 years, there has been a huge growth in the number of Buddhist teachers who are active in the West, in the number of Buddhist centers, and in the vast amount of books and tapes on the subject.

Why do you think Westerners, particularly younger Western-ers, have gravitated toward Buddhism in this way?

There are a number of reasons. Buddhism is seen as a spiritu-al tradition that is free from many of the rather uncomfortable trap-pings of traditional religion. A belief in God or Christ is not required in order to begin practicing Buddhism. Instead, Buddhism addresses the immediacy of each individual's experi-ence. Buddhism starts with the recognition that life contains pain and suffering, and not just physical pain, but a kind of spiritual malaise, an anxiety, a sense of meaninglessness. This analysis of the human condition is not presented as a kind of dogma, but as something for consideration. The tools for that consideration—meditation, reflection, and various other practices—enable us to look deeply into our own experience in such a way that we get a firsthand encounter with life, and in a way, perhaps, that offers greater clarity and depth than we would have otherwise had.

Buddhism then goes on to explain how we can live all aspects of our life—our ethical life, our spiritual life, our economic life—in such a way that we become increasingly aware of the nature of our existence. We can gain a deeper understanding of those habits and patterns of the mind that cause us to repeatedly give ourselves pain. It can lead to greater sensitivity, wisdom, compassion, and love. In the context of a practice, it is something we can actually do. The test of Buddhist practice is not that we conform to some rigid belief system, but that we actually free ourselves from what restricts us in our own lives. It's the practicality of Buddhism, the incisiveness of its philosophy and psychology, that has drawn a lot of people who have experienced a spiritual crisis in the West. To some Westerners, this tradition seems to be alive in a way that many aspects of Christianity are not.

There are a number of people trained in Catholicism who have come to Buddhism—particularly Tibetan Buddhism. Are the parallels in terms of comprehensiveness of each religion a reason for that?

It is very interesting to speculate on what kind of people are drawn to which kinds of Buddhism. I don't think anybody's really studied it, but certainly we are attracted to those forms of Buddhism that somehow have resonances with our own culture. Buddhism is neither a denial the West nor a denial of Christianity. It is simply a system of methods and of ways of living that allow us to fulfill those intuitions and feelings that aren't being fulfilled elsewhere. Some people find that through Buddhism they are actually brought back to Christianity. They find that through their meditation practice, they get an insight into what the Gospels really mean. I don't think Buddhism is concerned about converting the world to Buddhism. It's concerned with freeing the mind and opening up the potentials that the mind can contain. It's about reducing suffering in the world. It doesn't really matter if you are a Buddhist, a Christian, or something else.

The Buddhist teachers who have come to the West should not really be considered missionaries, but how should they be viewed?

One has to recognize that we are dealing with human beings here, and there are almost as many approaches to Buddhism as there are teachers. You have people such as the Dalai Lama who are certainly not interested in converting others to Buddhism. But some Buddhist organizations are quite explicitly missionary in nature. They do seek to convert people to Buddhism and to have them become card-carrying Buddhists of a certain school. So one has to be discerning. One has to try to break out of the habit of wanting to reduce something that is foreign and unknown into simple stereotypes. Such simplification might seem to make Buddhist concepts easier to handle, but, in fact, it only conceals the complexity, the richness, and the diversity of what is actually going on.

We should really speak of "Buddhism" as a plural— "Buddhisms." Perhaps we should even challenge the very concept of an "ism." After all, there is no equivalent term in any Asian language for "Buddhism." Buddhists talk of the "dharma," and dharma is one of these notorious words that eludes translation. It's a term that one understands only through living according to the values of Buddhist tradition, and then one begins to get a feel for what "dharma" is. Buddhists are concerned about people living in accordance with the dharma.

It is interesting to speculate about what the Buddha would say if he were here today. Would he speak of reincarnation and karma and those very Asian ideas? Or would he simply adopt the metaphors, the languages, and the ideas that resonate with people today? I suspect the latter. I don't think the Buddha would be interested in supporting what we now call Buddhism.

The Buddha—although he was a historical person—has meaning for Buddhists because he embodied a certain realization, a certain understanding, about life and death. That type of understanding is not exclusive to the historical figure of Buddha, but it is an open possibility for anyone, anywhere. Anyone who has, to some degree, embodied the state of enlightenment that the Buddha himself attained is challenged to find a means of articulating that understanding in a way that is comprehensible, meaningful, and accessible to you and me—to anybody in the world who is concerned about issues of meaning. So the challenge of Buddhism is finding a language that speaks to the modern world. I wouldn't limit it to the West. We are in an increasingly globalized culture, and the challenge of Buddhism is to become global, and not to retain, with any strong attachment, its identification with Tibet or Japan or the Theravada or the Mahayana or any of these schools.

How would a global Buddhism incorporate the ancient traditions, particularly the Tibetan traditions, that go back thousands of years? The prayers and mantras, for example, have been said over and over again for centuries. Are you suggesting that perhaps these will need to be discarded at some point, and something new will emerge out of the contemporary moment?

That would not necessarily be the case. Each time Buddhism has entered into a new culture (and it has done so many times), it has brought with it a body of practices, a philosophy, and a way of understanding the world in a certain way. This, of course, has to be preserved for there to be a recognizable continuity of the dharma—of the Buddhist tradition. The balancing act always requires retaining that which is essential, and discarding what is merely a cultural accretion—that which may have been valuable in Tibet or China or Japan, but is not really relevant any longer to the kind of world we live in today. So the big question really becomes: "What is essential?" Perhaps the continuity of reciting certain mantras, initiations, and so on does embody something very essential, something that cannot be altered without losing meaning. These are questions that can't be easily answered because we're talking about a process of interaction that is organic in nature. We need to plant the seeds in the soil of the world today, nurture them, and see which ones thrive and which ones don't. It's not really our business to be dogmatic about it, saying, "Well, this has to go, and this has to stay."

It may take several generations for this transition to occur. Historically, Buddhism has taken from 300 to 400 years to be assimilated into a new culture—so that we can actually differentiate between Chinese Buddhism and Tibetan Buddhism, for example. The transplantation of Buddhism is much more akin to the transplantation of a large tree. We may have all of these sophisticated information technologies, and we can learn a lot of facts about Buddhism more rapidly than ever before; nonetheless, the actual growth of a culture as complex as that of Buddhism cannot be rushed. It's a question of organic growth that might take generations. It needs to be passed through and processed by successive peoples over long periods of time. We also have to accept the idea that it might not take root. All we can do is our best and be truthful to that.

Earlier you mentioned that your training was done in the Gelug tradition. A lot of people probably aren't aware that there are a number of different schools of Buddhist thought. For example, there are four main schools of thought in Tibetan Buddhism. You describe the Gelug as scholarly. How would you describe the Nyingma, the Sakya, and the Kagyu?

I think one has to acknowledge that all the schools of Tibetan Buddhism contain the same basic elements. They all have scholarly traditions, and they all have what one might call contemplative traditions, or practice traditions. The differences are really a question of emphasis, which has evolved over time. Kagyu and Nyingma would generally be considered the more practice-oriented traditions. In other words, they would agree with the Gelug that you need to have a clear understanding of what you are doing before you do it, but they would also say that you don't need to spend 20 years getting that understanding. If you spend four or five years getting a clear grasp of these things, then the thing to do is to go into formal meditation practice—into long retreats. The Sakya is perhaps somewhere between the two, having a very strong scholarly tradition, as does the Gelug. Much of the Gelug's own scholarship, in fact, is derived from the Sakya tradition. But these traditions, especially recently, have an equally strong meditative tradition as well.

Paradoxically, the Chinese invasion of Tibet brought the wonders of Tibetan Buddhism to the West and the rest of the world. It is hard to believe that these treasures were locked up for over 1,000 years in the wilds of Tibet and insulated from the rest of the world. If not for this tragedy, we might still be in the same situation. What about that paradox? What is your view?

History is full of these ironies, and this is one of the greater ones. Tibet served as a kind of cold storage where the Buddhism of India, which had similarly been obliterated by the invading Muslim armies of the 12th century, was preserved. But perhaps it was too rigidly preserved. Tibet sought to cut itself off too much from the rest of the world, and perhaps its own craving for seclusion was one of the causes of its downfall. The two are not unlinked.

Tibet made a few attempts in the 1920s and 1930s to connect with the rest of the world, but it was too late by then. The Dalai Lama himself has said that Tibetans themselves are largely to blame for this. There was a good window of opportunity from 1912 to 1947 in which international relations could have been established. There could have been more of an outgoing policy, but this was resisted by the monks, the abbots, and the aristocracy who felt that any incursions into the outside world would despoil those very treasures that they preserved. It was a dilemma. They were probably right. If the outside world had come into Tibet in any form, it would have changed the situation. But the reality was that medieval Tibet could no longer survive in the modern geopolitical environment. Something was going to change. Unfortunately, what happened was a disaster of a major order. The people who did come in, the Chinese, came with extreme policies of cultural revolution, which led to an overwhelming destruction of Tibetan culture. There were 6,000 monasteries in 1959. By the end of the Cultural Revolution in 1976, there were only about 13 that hadn't been either completely destroyed or seriously desecrated and damaged. So, they did suffer enormously, and 1.2 million Tibetans lost their lives in this struggle. It is a huge tragedy in the world today, and one, unfortunately, that the West does not seem prepared to rectify.

When the Tibetans were being taken over by the Chinese, the Korean conflict was unfolding, and that captured the rest of the world's attention. We also didn't want to upset the Chinese too much. Were these valid reasons for the West's inattention?

The bottom line, really, is that it was not in anybody's interest economically or politically to come to the aid of Tibet. Tibet had nothing the rest of the world wanted. There was no real political motive to do anything, and also the sheer inaccessibility of the place played a part.

What do you see the future being for Buddhism as this encounter with the West continues?

It's very tempting to speculate as to what is going to unfold, but on the other hand, the future is, by definition, open. I remember a Tibetan lama was once asked, "What will be my future life?" And the lama said, "It's very easy to find that out. Look into your present state of mind, and there you will see your future." That is also true on a broader scale. If we want to see what kind of Buddhism is going to emerge in the West, we have to see what we are doing now. We have to see to what extent we really are committed, and to what extent we're not motivated by egoism or other personal or political agendas. We need to see that the quality of our own practice as Buddhists will be the foundation on which the future unfolds.

The responsibility is very much in the hands of those of us who are practicing Buddhism today. Buddhism does not exist apart from that. It's not some ethereal entity wending its way through history. It continues through the individuals who practice it. That is what will determine the future. I hope it brings greater qualities of wisdom and compassion into the world and that it helps heal some of our global ills. That is my hope. But whether it will or not depends on the quality of our own lives now.

❖❖❖

EPILOGUE

Stephen Batchelor helps us to place Buddhism in both a historical and geographical context relative to other spiritual traditions. We begin to see that the contemporary present we experience is the result of centuries of interaction, hostility, and struggle. Of course, in the process of spreading Western scientific materialism throughout the globe, we have, in some sense, traded our souls for the illusion of security and material wealth. At the same time, we have lost our spiritual rudder and are drifting without any clear direction.

Without becoming Buddhists, we can still benefit from its principles and commonsense wisdom, whatever our spiritual persuasion may be. The fact that for centuries Buddhist wisdom has entered many different regions and countries, has adapted to the local environment, and has been assimilated over time while incorporating the cultural aspects of its environment, speaks to its universal appeal.

❖❖❖ ❖❖❖

CHAPTER FIVE

Dharma Wisdom

Kalu Rinpoche
and Michael Toms

PROLOGUE

*F*or 2,500 years, the message of Buddhism has been clear
and amazingly consistent. The dharma has entered many
cultures and adapted itself without compromise. Since the exo-
dus of tens of thousands of Tibetans after the Chinese invasion
in 1959, the world has been the beneficiary of the Tibetan
approach to the Buddhist tradition. One of the most respected
teachers in Tibetan Buddhism to have come to the West was the
late venerable Kalu Rinpoche (1905–1989). His latest incarnation was discovered shortly after Kalu's death and is now undergoing training at Sonada Monastery in India. Kalu established
dharma centers throughout Europe, North America, and
Canada, while making his home at Sonada Monastery in India.
He also established the first three-year solitary retreat program
in the West. The following interview was conducted in early

1987 after a Red Chenrezig empowerment ritual given by Kalu Rinpoche in San Francisco.

❖❖❖

MICHAEL TOMS: *In the late 1950s, when China invaded Tibet, it forced many people to leave the country. The exiles went first to India, and then began to move to other parts of the world. That created another phenomenon; that is, bringing the message of Tibetan Buddhism to America and the rest of the world. How do you see that transition and its relevance, and what do you see as the impact of Tibetan Buddhism on America?*

KALU RINPOCHE: Prior to the military occupation of Tibet, the society was, to a great extent, very peaceful and happy. It offered stability, prosperity, and a decent standard of living to all the people in the society. But at a certain point, there was a kind of degeneration, or a kind of breaking apart, of the social fabric of the Tibetans. Moral qualities and virtuous actions that had been previously held in high regard by the culture tended to fall away. People began to forget these important parts of living a good life and being good citizens of the society. And people became more and more involved in negative and disruptive kinds of behavior. To a large extent, this was a kind of karmic process, in that the misfortunes that befell Tibet were due to the karma of the people themselves. It was due to this disintegration of the moral fabric of Tibetan culture that the catastrophe came about. When the Chinese began to make inroads into Tibet in the 1950s, the Tibetan people were divided in their opinion. There were many who felt that this was a welcome thing, and there would be nothing but benefits. The Chinese, of course, were careful to encourage this impression. There were many people, however, who were convinced that this would mean nothing but bad things for the Tibetan people and their culture.

When the hostilities finally broke out in eastern Tibet, in the area we know as Kham—which was my home—I was convinced that for someone like myself, who was a practitioner of dharma and interested basically in spiritual practice, such a disruptive situation was not going to be beneficial at all. I didn't feel that I had enough political influence or power to stop the hostilities, so I left my home and went to the capital of Lhasa in central Tibet. From there, I made my way to the neighboring country of Bhutan. It was there that I set about building up a monastery that already existed in Bhutan. While I was outside Tibet, the final uprising took place, and the military occupation by the Chinese came about.

At that point, of course, a number of Tibetans who had been totally opposed to the inroads that the Chinese were making decided to flee their country and become refugees in countries such as India and Nepal, bordering the Tibetan region. The vast majority of people who remained behind had made the decision to take the consequences, and in many cases they endured a very hellish oppression under the Chinese forces. A great deal of misfortune came about because of this. The refugees, however, took with them one of the most important things in their lives, and that was their faith and involvement in the practice of Buddhism. In fact, among their numbers were many spiritual teachers, lamas, and others directly involved in the tradition and practice of the meditative disciplines.

At that time, the Tibetan people did not have much understanding of, or contact with, the West. It is again my belief that these contacts came about due to previous karmic connections from other lifetimes that were manifesting in this particular lifetime. In my own particular case, while I was in India, I met a young American who became a student of mine and who, in fact, sponsored my first tour of North America and Europe. It was he who felt that my coming to the West would be beneficial.

When I arrived in America in 1971, the venerable Chögyam Trungpa Rinpoche, another teacher of our particular school, the Kagyu school, had already come to America from the United Kingdom. He was involved in establishing Buddhist centers, and his approach was to present American Buddhism rather than teach traditional Buddhism. He would present concepts from an American perspective and gradually introduce people to fundamental concepts. He was particularly skillful in this approach, introducing the teachings in a way that American people would find much more understandable. I was convinced, however, that in the short time I would be there, what I needed to do was to teach Buddhism as I understood it—as I understood the Buddha to have taught it—as thoroughly and effectively as possible in each and every situation. My goal was to plant as many seeds as I could.

On that occasion, I was not able to actually found very many centers, but my subsequent trips were more successful. This is my fourth trip to North America, and I've not been the only teacher of the Tibetan tradition by any means. A number of other teachers from all four schools of the Tibetan Buddhist tradition—the Gelug, Kagyu, Nyingma, and Sakya schools—have been instrumental in founding a number of centers in the West and throughout the world. As for my own experience, during my four trips, I have been able to establish more than 70 centers throughout the world. If we take the Kagyu School with which I'm affiliated as an example of the now widespread development of Tibetan Buddhism in the West, we find that there are some 325 centers associated with this tradition alone—which is merely one of the four.

All four schools have found Westerners to be very responsive to the teachings that Buddhism offers. This is due not only to the blessings and profundity of the teachings themselves, but also due in great part to the intelligence and awareness of the people in these countries. They are sincerely seeking the kinds of answers that Buddhism can provide, and they have the intelligence to understand the import of its profound teachings. In my own experience, I have found that the connection between the teachings of Buddhism and the people in the West has been very strong, and there has been quite a positive response.

These are challenging times that we live in. What does your path of Buddhism offer people in these times?

The most beneficial and important thing for people to understand is the nature of mind. Based upon this understanding, people need to develop love and compassion for each other. We have to learn to be kind in the way that nurturing parents are kind. And we have to learn to express our gratitude for that kindness to all living beings. This attitude will naturally give rise to love and compassion for all creatures.

We have to recognize that suffering arises from the mind, and then we have to know the mind's true nature. By recognizing that the mind's true nature is emptiness, then we can recognize that all suffering is emptiness; thereby, we alleviate suffering.

The mind is a tricky instrument. Many of us don't even know that we are suffering when we are. Sometimes we rationalize and fool ourselves. What are ways to move into this empty mind that will allow us to become more aware of what's actually going on?

To recognize that the mind's nature is emptiness, it is best to refer to the example of the dream. While in a dream state, we have the experience of thinking that the dream is real. We may experience a great deal of suffering in the dream. We may experience pain, anger, or any number of different emotional reactions to the dream because we believe this dream is real. But if we recognize that the dream is only a dream even while we are having it, and if we recognize that this dream is a manifestation of the mind's true nature of being essentially emptiness, then we don't have that emotional reaction to the dream experience.

Our daily experience can be understood in the same way. Life is as unreal as a dream. The appearances of the dream state and the after-death state are the same in that these appearances arise from the mind's nature.

Over the last two or three decades, there have been many teachings and disciplines that have come to the West—particularly to the United States. And there have been a great many teachings focusing on the practice of meditation. What do you feel about the relevance and importance of meditation in today's world?

One reason that there has been such an influx of religious traditions in America and the West is because these countries offer great freedom and have populations with varied religious needs. It is possible for many different religious traditions to spread in such an environment.

Another reason that Buddhism has flourished in the West is because this life experience is so hectic, and Buddhism offers hope of inner peace. In the West, people are always active, they have to talk constantly, and their minds are always filled with discursive thought. Most people become thoroughly exhausted by this. Out of this exhaustion, people have the hope that by meditating, they can experience some peace and happiness.

Among the different Buddhist traditions, a variety of systems and methods exist for meditation, all of which are good. All of them are the beneficial activity of the Buddha, and the different traditions correlate to the different acumen and qualities of the individual. Another name for a Buddhist is an inner practitioner—a Trungpa, as it's called in Tibet. It's called "inner" because the methods of meditation and the actual practice and path of the inner practitioner are those that benefit the mind, bringing realization and bliss. Accordingly, a number of methods exist that are extremely profound, extremely vast, and very powerful; they all offer a means of bringing about this realization.

Within this inner path of Buddhism, then, by means of bringing great peace and happiness to the mind, the body and the speech also become filled with bliss and happiness. So this inner path of Buddhism doesn't have any external work that needs to be done. It doesn't prescribe an external, worldly type of activity. However, because this dharma has to flourish and be propagated within a worldly environment—that is, in a society—we need the various dharma centers in order to provide a certain basis in worldly activity. Because the dharma centers need to support a resident lama, they need to have a building. They need to participate in a limited amount of worldly activity. The dharma center actually combines the worldly activity and the inner path.

Some people have taken the principle of right living—particularly in America—and translated or presumed it to mean bringing one's practice into daily life. How do you see the idea of right living as bringing one's practice or discipline into daily life? Is it possible to do so, particularly in a contemporary society such as America?

If you develop a deep understanding of the nature of mind and have great diligence and energy with that understanding, then it can be combined with worldly action—with one's livelihood.

There are many methods for bringing about this unification of one's practice with ordinary worldly activity. For instance, the first thing we all do in the morning is wake up and get out of bed. At that moment of waking up, we need to remember and recognize that on this day all sentient beings are kindly parents, and we will commit our lives and actions to the benefit of others. We need to say, "May all that I do on this day be beneficial to everyone who has contact with me." And in so thinking, we give rise to an altruistic attitude. Further, by recognizing that all appearance, all experience, is like a dream or a reflection in the mirror—having no substantial reality—then with that recognition, we can diminish our emotional distractions. We can diminish feelings of irritation and craving, of anger and lust, and so on. In turn, we can fortify and increase our feelings of love and compassion, and then apply ourselves to whatever worldly work is necessary.

The pinnacle teachings of the Mahamudra involve meditating on the mind's true nature and on the mind's essence. This teaching also involves recognizing that everything is dharma. All worldly experience can be thought of as a journey down a path. There are things we notice on our travels, but we always stay on the path. This is the Mahamudra practice. How is experience part of the path? Experience is what we see, what we hear, what we taste, what we touch, and so on. This is what is meant by experience. When experiencing form, for example, we see it. We see that the form is form void. When we experience sounds, the sound is sound void. Taste is taste void. Touch is feeling void. All thoughts and concepts are just the brilliance of awareness void.

For instance, once in India there was a local king who ruled over a large area. He was completely absorbed with the office of his kingdom. One day, the king received the pointing out instructions, or Mahamudra, on the nature of mind. He understood the concept, and without giving up any of his royal duties, in 12 years attained complete enlightenment. In the same way, if a great politician in America were to receive this instruction on the nature of mind and were able to meditate with that instruction, then such a politician would attain enlightenment by manipulating politics.

Here's another example. In Tibet, there lived the great Marpalotsawa, who was not an ordained person. He had several wives and many children; he enjoyed drinking beer and running his household. By realizing Mahamudra and applying the Mahamudra to all his activity, he became a completely realized Siddha who was able to manifest any miracle and encountered absolutely no obstruction to whatever miraculous appearance was required to be manifested.

These stories serve to point out that if we receive this instruction and meditate on it, actually realize it, then we, too, can reach enlightenment—whatever our position in life.

Is it necessary to have a spiritual teacher? If so, why?

It is necessary to have a spiritual guide. Without one you cannot learn how to meditate; you cannot receive the instruction on how to meditate.

It is not difficult to choose a spiritual guide. First, it's based upon a liking. You just feel a connection, and you feel that liking within your mind. But the spiritual guide must have great love and compassion. The guide must be one who is able to first give beginning instruction, and as your experience increases, the guide must be able to lead you forward on the path. That's the quality of the spiritual guide. By first liking the guide and then receiving the teachings, you will find that this is really beneficial. And by feeling the benefits, you will think of your teacher as extremely kind, so you will develop great gratitude. As the instructions increase and your experience increases, you realize it is more than gratitude. It is great devotion, great faith, because you will see that the spiritual guide is leading you on the path to complete liberation.

You need to stay with the spiritual teacher until you have received all the instruction, developed understanding, and learned how to practice the instruction. Once that has taken place, then the instruction becomes the only spiritual guide you need.

You mentioned previously that a great many disciplines and teachings have come to the West. If one looks at Buddhism, particularly from an outsider's point of view, it seems there are many, many schools of Buddhism. If one compares Zen and Tibetan Buddhism, for example, there seem to be many differences. Could you speak to those differences as well as to the common ground?

The differences in the various aspects of Buddhism are in accordance with the differences in the acumen of various types of people. For instance, some people need to practice the Hinayana teaching, because on hearing the profound teachings of the Mahayana, they would become afraid. But they have the extremely noble and very wonderful path of the Hinayana to follow, and that is very fitting for their particular attitude. Those who have slightly larger scope, larger vision, can conceive of the extremely vast and profound ideas of the Mahayana. They will find the Hinayana a poor fit. So those people need to practice Mahayana. Then, there are others who are completely convinced of the extreme profundity and power of the Vajrayana, and they want to practice that. So the different schools of Buddhism are there to accommodate the different requirements of individuals.

Within Tibetan Buddhism there are four different schools of thought: Gelug, Kagyu, Nyingma, and Sakya. What are the differences among those four, and why do they exist as separate sects?

All the traditions in Tibet are the same in that they are all the profound, wonderful teachings of the Buddha. The differences in naming these various schools is comparable to the different state names in the United States of America. The names are different, but they are all states. It is that kind of division. When the dharma was brought into Tibet from India by various individuals—with individual names—the various lineages took on, to a certain extent, the name of the one who brought in the dharma. Each school is associated with that person from India. However, they are all the teachings of the Buddha, containing complete teachings of the Sutra and the Tantra. If you were to say that these four are exactly the same, this would be incorrect, because there are some differences. Think of the differences as factories that produce vehicles for traveling. Some will produce cars, some will produce trains, airplanes, and so on. It is this kind of difference.

In the 1960s, there was the emergence of the ecumenical movement in Christianity, but it was predated in Tibet by the Rime movement. What is the Rime tradition, and what is its significance and relationship to the ecumenical movement in Christianity?

In Tibet, there is the Rime or nonsectarian school that you may loosely translate as ecumenical. My teacher and several of his colleagues were involved and were Rime lamas. In the previous incarnation of my teacher, the great Kongtrul Rinpoche, a most amazing, wonderful lama, unified the eight great traditions. Thinking in a very nonsectarian way, he studied and gave many talks on this nonsectarian viewpoint. He also wrote many books on each of the schools from this nonsectarian viewpoint, and established the Rime tradition.

All dharmas are Buddhist dharmas. All dharmas are the same essence. So it is definitely very good to have this nonsectarian view. But it's also good to have a sectarian view. One can either be nonsectarian and interested in developing an understanding of all traditions, or one can be sectarian and completely whole in one tradition. The benefits are equal, especially because within the world, people are subject to a great number of emotional distractions, different reactions to things, and to pride and jealousy. By being sectarian, you actually put that pride and jealousy to use and turn it into the thing that propagates the dharma. Jealousy makes you see that some other tradition is developing and doing very well, and then pride makes you want your tradition to do well. So you make that pride and jealousy do the work of propagating the dharma, which is absolutely pure, and therefore you are doing something useful.

Both of these methods are fine. You can decide definitely on one path, or you can consider all paths and take a little from each. The first method is definitely easier because you only have to navigate one path, and you are convinced that through this path you can attain enlightenment if you just go straight on the path. The other method of taking a little from each path will eventually help you reach enlightenment, but the travel time is longer; it is not so direct. Say you want to get to India. The first method is to take a direct flight from America and land in India. The second method is to take a flight from America, land somewhere, and then take a car. After driving for a long time in the car, you get on a boat. Eventually you will reach your destination.

Is there anything you would like to discuss that you haven't as yet touched upon?

The teachings of the Buddha are in no way harmful. It is not a teaching that instructs us to give up the world, abandon the world. The teachings of the Buddha are beneficial in all senses. There are the extremely profound and vast teachings in medicine, philosophy, semantics, languages, astrology, and so on. These teachings need to be understood by people. Even if we are not able to develop great understanding and great realization in this lifetime, we must encourage the growth of this seed of faith and develop our practice of virtue. Developing our understanding as much as we can will be extremely beneficial, not only in this lifetime, but in all future lifetimes.

❖❖❖

EPILOGUE

Here, the late Kalu Rinpoche brings us back to the nature of mind and its relevance to cutting through the illusions preventing us from seeing what is real and what isn't. As one of the major Tibetan teachers of the 20th century, his wisdom is especially noteworthy when he addresses the inner and outer, and how we can accomplish balance between our internal and external experience and practice. The benefits of a spiritual teacher, differences in the various schools of Buddhism, ecumenical Buddhism, and more are covered as he gives us the blessings of his wide experience and understanding of Buddhist philosophy.

❖❖❖ ❖❖❖

CHAPTER SIX

Zen
Ethics

Robert Aitken Roshi
and Michael Toms

PROLOGUE

*W*ithin the maze of social and political processes of our society, we can easily lose our way. How do we maintain our
center and personal integrity in the midst of great chaos and confusion? The Buddhist tradition has some pertinent things to say in
response to this question. In the following discussion, Robert
Aitken Roshi will explore how the individual can grow spiritually
while living in society. Aitken Roshi is the former director of the
Diamond Sangha and teacher at its two centers, Koko An Zendo
and Maui Zendo, in Hawaii. Retired now, he is a founding member and past president of the Buddhist Peace Fellowship. Aitken
Roshi is also the author of Taking the Path of Zen, The Mind of
Clover, *and* The Practice of Perfection.

❖❖❖

MICHAEL TOMS: In your book The Mind of Clover, *the first ten chapters deal with the ten grave precepts. Perhaps you can start there and describe some of those precepts. What are they? Where did they come from?*

ROBERT AITKEN ROSHI: The precepts grew out of Shakyamuni Buddha's original teachings and have been developed and refined throughout the centuries by the various cultures through which Buddhism has passed. The ten so-called grave precepts are a development in Mahayana Buddhism, that is to say, northern Buddhism, which originated in India but developed in China, Korea, and Japan. These precepts are taught in Zen Buddhism as koans, or as themes of meditation at the end of koan practice. But they are also well known to Zen Buddhists—and all Buddhists—as guides for everyday behavior.

You do not have to be a Buddhist, however, to use these precepts. They are not commandments inscribed in stone, but rather they are natural ways of ordinary human practice that help us find fulfillment. They are not based on any idea of right and wrong, but on ideas of what is correct and incorrect, or ignorant and wise.

Why are the precepts particularly relevant to contemporary times? They've been around for hundreds of years, so why should we pay attention to them now?

We have allowed expedience to take a primary place in our judgments, particularly in our wider social and political judgments, and we've forgotten the important values of conservation and protection of all beings. Since the 1960s, thoughtful people have been searching for values that will enable them to find their way in these confused times when our political leaders seem to be interested only in the expedient ways. The ten grave precepts offer guidance in this area.

In China, Korea, and Japan, Buddhists were also influenced by Confucian standards of behavior, which involved loyalty to the superior and responsibility to the inferior. However, Buddhism in this country has left Confucianism behind, and we are faced with koans that may not be so meaningful for beginning or even intermediate Zen students. Therefore, the precepts are not generally taught in Zen centers, although some lip service is paid to them. People agree to accept the precepts when they decide to take formal vows as Buddhists, but they are not generally discussed in detail in public talks or even in interviews with teachers. So it's my concern that we give more attention to the precepts and understand their origins and how they apply to our lives now. For example, we need to understand the significance of the literal injunction not to kill, but we also need to understand the significance of the compassionate aspect not to kill so that we can give life to others, and understand the significance of the absolute aspect that there is no killing in the mind.

In the Judeo-Christian culture, we think of killing in terms of killing animals and other human beings. We don't think particularly about our effect on the environment, but in a sense, what we are doing now is killing parts of the environment.

When we look closely at the word *beings*, in both Asian and Western languages, we find that beings are not limited to that which we ordinarily consider sentient. Indeed, storms, clouds, unicorns, and so on are beings. So the precept not to kill is really a fulfillment of our vow to save all beings, and the protection of the environment is an essential part of that vow.

I'm very sympathetic to the deep ecology movement, which rejects, for example, the attitude of mere stewardship in the forests, and of harvesting animals, plants, and trees. Instead, this ecological movement encourages the forest to be itself, or a jungle to be itself, and to fulfill itself in the same way that we hope to encourage human beings to fulfill themselves. When we look at the long history of evolution, we find that the era of human beings is only a tiny portion of that vast spectrum. Who knows what is going to evolve out of this wonderful nature with its rich variety of beings? And who are we to manipulate things with our short heritage just for our own extremely limited ends? What about the porpoise? The scientists who work with porpoises, trying to teach them how to do things our way, find that the porpoises are trying to teach the scientists what their way is. And they are delighted when it becomes evident that the scientists can actually repeat the same sounds the porpoises make.

You mention the idea of fulfilling ourselves, which brings up the question of self and who it is that's being fulfilled. There seems to be some misunderstanding about the nature of self when it comes to Buddhism. Could you address that issue?

There is a popular idea among people who encounter Asian religion and New Age subjects that somehow we must get rid of ourselves. I think this is a great misunderstanding. It is not possible to get rid of one's self. It is possible, however, to forget one's self, and this is what Buddhists seek to do. I tell students frequently that Shakyamuni Buddha had a big ego; that is, he knew very well who he was and what he had to do. He had a very clear sense of himself.

If we have a clear sense of ourselves, we are more readily able to take up religious studies. If one is still in a kind of adolescent stage of working out career matters, courtship matters, and so on, trying to figure out who one is in a social way, then it's rather difficult to focus on deeper questions. I liken this to the athlete on the high board who has trained for a long time and is completely confident in her ability to make a perfect dive. The diver can forget about herself, and just allow her body to perform the familiar task. But it is really only possible to forget one's self when one has a good understanding of what that self is and what it can accomplish.

Forgetting the self is a momentary experience. It's what St. Paul called putting off the old man and putting on the new man. He uses the word *man* there, or at least the translators do. It would be true also for putting on the new woman, taking off the old woman. Dharmalaksana, the founder of Soto Zen Buddhism in Japan, used the expression "body and mind fall away." "Slough away" is another way to translate that—as in sloughing away the old skin of a snake. It's very much like St. Paul's expression. This ability comes with rigorous and directed meditative practice.

In the West, particularly in America, we seem to be on a quest for more and more knowledge. You can walk into the average corner bookstore and literally be exposed to the great teachings of all time in the form of paperback books. It is a reflection of our society in the sense that we've become collectors of teachings. What do you think about the tendency that we have to collect teachings?

It's not as pronounced a tendency as it was 20 to 25 years ago, when commonly, each teacher would encounter people who were scrapbook practitioners. These are practitioners who wanted to be able to say, "Well, I sat with such-and-such Roshi and so-and-so Rinpoche, and I met so-and-so guru." They literally pasted the teachers' names and pictures in their scrapbooks. But people are coming more and more to understand that, in the words of a teacher I admire, "You don't strike water by starting new wells." It is important to find the place where you are most comfortable and stay there. It is also important to find the teacher with whom you feel most compatible.

It's easy to fool one's self with experiences of no real significance and to be carried off on byways. So it's important to have a teacher who is clear-eyed, who has gone through the experience of forgetting himself, and has trained thereafter to the point where he can really devote himself fully to the student. It is necessary for the teacher to hold up the ancient mirror to the student to show that each of us is really the Buddha from the beginning. It is quite possible for us to put off preoccupations and preconceptions and go our own way, standing on our own two feet.

There is also the idea of the guru within, or the teacher within. How does that correspond to the relationship of teacher and student?

Of course, the teacher within is important. In Zen terms, we are born alone, we die alone, and we have realization alone. So the teacher, really, is one who stands to one side. The teacher does not wear the face of God, but is rather a dharma guide, or a spiritual friend. The guide helps us turn back on ourselves and out into the community, the society, the world—the Universe. The guide helps us keep our experience in perspective, helping us understand that the experience is an interesting and important milestone. As we turn a little bit in one direction and encourage ourselves to go that way, we find another milestone.

You use the term "face of God." There is typically a Western misunderstanding about God in Buddhist terms. What is God in Buddhism?

The term is not used, of course. There are many archetypes. The Bodhisattvas are archetypes that can be compared with saints or angels. These archetypes are important for Buddhists because they illuminate our path. For example, the Kuan Yin Bodhisattva, or Avalokiteshvara, known as Kannon in Japanese, is the embodiment of mercy and compassion. The name literally means "the one who hears the sound of suffering in the world," or "the one who hears the sounds of the world." Hearing those sounds, Kannon is one with all beings, not in a static way, but actually engaged compassionately with their suffering.

These archetypes are very important, and there are many in the Buddhist pantheon. But Dharmakaya, the body of the law, which is a very poor translation, really means "the vast and fathomless void that is full of possibilities, full of potential." This is what underlies us; this is what infuses us. But to give that a personal name is to put a kind of face on the void, and it obscures the fathomless, infinite, and rich nature of it. We find this same kind of tradition in the West in Christianity and in Judaism, with its strong reluctance in deeper traditions to stay away from naming God.

How would you compare Jesus Christ and Gautama Buddha? How would you relate the two as personages?

Each rose from within his own culture and was obliged to use the cultural terms and traditions of his culture. And each stepped beyond his own culture to some degree—although you can see the Buddhist teaching when you look closely at the Upanishads, and you can see the old Jewish teachers' instructions in Jesus' words. But Jesus and Gautama Buddha used the old terms in a new way. Even though they were products of their respective cultures in many ways, they were still enlightened beings. I use the words of Jesus often in my teaching. And some good Christian teachers I know will frequently quote the Buddha or some of the founding teachers in the Buddhist faith.

Jesus may even have been influenced by some of those Buddhist traders who crossed the Holy Land centuries before he walked there. And, of course, there was a good deal of cross-fertilization after his death. Until more research is done in this area, it is rather risky to conjecture about the hidden years of Jesus' career. You remember many years ago there was a book called *The Hidden Years*, which purported to examine what he went through during that time. Some Buddhists will tell you that he went to India, but no one really knows.

The whole idea of bringing Zen values into the world and into the social and political milieu is almost contrary to the monastic tradition of Zen, where one goes off to the temple and essentially just practices Zen to the exclusion of everything else. There is no mixing with the outside world. What about that?

The heritage of Western Zen Buddhism is monastic, and it has a kind of complicated history beginning with the time of Shakyamuni Buddha himself. In Indian culture, despite the fact that there is the strong Advaita tradition of nondualism, there is still a separation in people's minds of this world from the "other-world." So the monks and nuns tended to cloister themselves in a way to cultivate themselves in the otherworld. But as the religion moved to China, Korea, and Japan, it encountered a "worldly" culture, where there was no real sympathy for an otherworldly view at all. In fact, the idea of a person being celibate was quite contrary to the Chinese view that it was important for the son or daughter to carry on the line by having a family. One would think that Buddhism might lose its otherworldly quality in China, but it did not because it was a guest religion. It was just there on sufferance.

For its own protection, it maintained the monastic structure and kept a low profile.

When Buddhism moved to this country, we inherited the monastic tradition and almost unconsciously maintained a quasi-monastic model in some centers, with many monks and nuns being ordained. Even in centers that consist of a completely lay fellowship, the members nonetheless have the idea that you must give up the world at least to some degree. Now, after 25 years or more of active work in the West, these Zen centers are trying to cultivate true "lay" Zen Buddhism. They want to find ways for the individual to take responsibility for the practice, rather than looking to a certain kind of building or a certain procedure to do so. In the course of this, we are concerned about teaching ways of practice in the home—of rituals in the home. We seek ways of teaching children about Buddhism and giving them a sense of what religion really is. We want to teach the precepts that were given a lot of lip service in the old monastic days, but the real standard was Confucianism. Now, we must make these precepts our own in a most intimate way. We must understand them clearly—not as commandments, but as expressions of our own Buddha nature.

What about the patriarchal quality that is associated with Zen?

This has been a source of much concern. In our own sangha in Hawaii, the women got together many years ago and just talked about the patriarchal nature of the heritage. They talked about the sexist language in the rituals and brought pressure to bear on me, showing me what I was saying, what I was doing— particularly with regard to language. It's interesting that in Chinese and Japanese, pronouns are not used nearly as much as they are in English. Things that are quite impersonal in the original language have tended to be translated in a sexist way that excludes women. So we went through all our materials and fixed all that quite satisfactorily.

Then the concern was, "Well, when we recite the names of all our teachers, they are all men. When we put up pictures of our teachers, they are all men. Weren't there any women back then?" We talked this over, and with some help, we researched and found stories in which women were teachers. Women were shown to be really enlightened. The women's collective that was started in Hawaii several years ago published these stories. We call them KaHawaii Koans, and they are entirely stories about women.

It is very interesting to see how teachers such as Joshu or JowJo, whom we know about only through their dialogues with monks, actually had many dialogues with women. It's important that we bring this out. It's also important that we show that although the culture has been sexist, and more or less prevented any of these women from becoming Roshis, there is nothing inherent in the religion that prevents such an occurrence. Now that Buddhism is in a more egalitarian society, women teachers can emerge, and indeed they are emerging.

When you refer to Buddhism as a religion, which of course it is, what is Zen within that context?

Zen is, in that context, one stream of Buddhism—one form of Buddhist religion. There is a tendency, I think, rising out of Dr. Suzuki's writings, although I don't think he would ever say it himself, that Zen is somehow self-improvement exercises, or a way of realizing true nature without regard to formal religion. It is my belief that Zen Buddhism is very much a religion, and that devotion is an important part of Zen practice.

You mention devotion, which brings up the question, "To whom does one devote oneself?" Devotion is a stumbling block for a lot of people because it seems to imply a surrender to something other than oneself. What is your response to that?

When we look at the way we use the word *religion* in ordinary terms, such as: "She studies religiously," we mean that she devotes herself to her work. She forgets herself in her work. This is an analogy for the kind of devotion that is necessary for true practice. I meet people from time to time who feel threatened by ritual and by the idea of devotion. Some of my older students—and maybe even I—reject some forms of devotion. I recall listening to a senior student introduce a new student to the practice of bowing. He said, "At this point, you bow to the wall." And I said, "Hey, wait a minute. You don't bow *to* the wall; you bow *toward* the wall." The meanings are quite different.

Bowing is the act of throwing everything away. It is also said that bowing to the floor is the act of raising the Buddha's feet over your head, and that's hard to take at first. I grew up in the '30s when every intelligent young person was a Marxist, or presumed that he or she was a Marxist, and then I found myself in a monastery not too long after that, bowing to the floor. *What am I doing?* I thought. And then I thought, *Well, these are just Buddhist exercises*, which is about the best I could come up with and still keep myself there.

It's difficult growing up in a humanist kind of environment and moving into a devotional one, but it is necessary that one gradually move toward a true spirit of devotion. It is important to realize that it is entirely possible to devote oneself to a teacher, a lineage, or a teaching and still keep a questioning spirit alive. It is still possible to say, "Hey, wait a minute. I don't think I agree with that. How about that?"

That is a salient point, because we have examples of spiritual communities in which the members didn't retain that questioning mind. They threw that facility away, and in so doing, somehow projected onto the teacher aspects that were clearly not there—or were illusions.

In *The Mind of Clover*, I tell about meeting a chap who was a disciple of a well-known Indian guru, and so I said that I liked some of the things I'd read in this man's book, but I found him both sexist and anti-Semitic. And he said, "Yes, it is true. I am sexist and anti-Semitic, but I am the guru." In my view, that won't do at all. I think it is possible to forget one's self completely, but at the same time, remain open so that anything that doesn't ring true will sound an alarm.

Any teaching can be perverted and misused, and Buddhism is one of them. I have heard it said about a certain teacher that he is so enlightened that he has transcended the precepts. Well, I think that's the kind of thing that could be used to justify any kind of criminal behavior. It is very dangerous.

When we talk about bringing these values into the real world, people often respond with anger. What about anger, and how do we deal with it?

It is very interesting that among the ten precepts, there is only one that deals with emotion—and that is the precept about anger. I myself have a hard time with this. In *The Mind of Clover*, I tell about meeting a Tibetan teacher. He asked me, "What do these young people say about anger?" And I said, "There is no anger—no one to get angry, and no one to get angry at." He gave me a very fishy look and said nothing more. When I stopped to think about it, I realized that all of my teachers had hot tempers, and I had felt the heat of those tempers on a number of occasions.

The question really becomes: "What is the nature of anger?" Is it possible to be impersonally angry? Children learn from the anger of their parents. When the anger is expressed directly, incisively, it comes across very cleanly, and there is no residue at all. The child responds immediately. But when the anger contains some personal concern for self-protection, for ego gratification, then it isn't clean, and you get some feedback. If you are sensitive to it, then you can say, "Wow, that was an expression of personal concern." It may be that the angry response will itself be clean, and you can respond in the way the child will respond. The child will get down from the ladder and not try to reach for whatever it is on the top shelf—he will not endanger himself in that way.

How would you extend that personal transformation of anger to the larger level, such as when dealing with weapons proliferation and nuclear arms?

It's a kind of energy. So if one does one's homework and knows the facts, one can discover what these weapons are and what their effect will be on a society diverting money into those weapons rather than into something more productive. With these facts at one's fingertips, one can deliver them with energy, and it will be very convincing because it will come across with passion.

Perhaps you can briefly address the idea of compassion. Again, there is a misinterpretation of it in some sense so that compassion becomes a sentimental idea and not one that involves passion. Certainly there is the exercise of passion within Buddhism.

When we look at the etymology of the word *passion*, we find that one of its meanings is "suffering." *Compassion* means to suffer with others. It is an expression of the fact that we are not limited by our skin. Each mind is the mind of the universe, and we are all working together for a better world.

❖❖❖

EPILOGUE

The freshness and clarity of the Zen perspective comes through in this dialogue with Robert Aitken Roshi, who uses the real world to present some of the most relevant Buddhist principles. He also delivers another view on the self and the misunderstanding surrounding its negation, according to the Buddhist perspective. In a delightful way, he addresses some of the critiques associated with Buddhism and provides some provocative responses. His insights about spiritual teachers and spiritual communities are especially appropriate. The final point he leaves us with is about anger and its relevance to the personal and planetary condition, followed once again by the ever-present Buddhist emphasis on compassion as the means to a peaceful world.

❖❖❖ ❖❖❖

CHAPTER SEVEN

Practicing Lovingkindness

Jack Kornfield and Michael Toms

PROLOGUE

*C*an I live fully? Do I live well? These are two of the greatest
spiritual questions we can ask. To look at how we have loved
and not loved, and the ways to nourish an open and joyful being
in the midst of daily life can serve as the means to propel us to
another deeper level of understanding ourselves. In the following
discussion, Jack Kornfield explores the nature of lovingkindness,
forgiveness, and compassion. He is one of those pioneers who has
brought the wisdom of Buddhism into American life over the past
two decades.

*Jack Kornfield was trained as a Buddhist monk in Thailand,
Burma, and India, and he has taught meditation worldwide since
1974. He was one of the key teachers to introduce Theravada
Buddhist practice to the West. For many years, his work has been
focused on integrating and bringing alive the great Eastern spiri-*

tual teachings in an accessible way for Western students. Jack also holds a Ph.D. in clinical psychology. He's a husband, father, psychotherapist, and founding teacher of the Insight Meditation Society and the Spirit Rock Center located in Woodacre, California. His books include Seeking the Heart of Wisdom, A Still Forest Pool, A Path with Heart, *and* Buddha's Little Instruction book. *He is co-author of* Soul Food *and the editor of* The Teachings of the Buddha.

❖❖❖

MICHAEL TOMS: *Many people have the idea that being spiritual or practicing spirituality means removing one's self from the problems and concerns of the world and going inside one's self and becoming self-absorbed. How accurate is that assessment?*

JACK KORNFIELD: Certainly in the complexity of our modern environment, we need time to be still and quiet, just as we breathe in and breathe out. Every wise culture knows that people need a retreat, a vacation, a day to be silent, to reconnect with themselves. But that does not at all portray the essence of spirituality. That's just a part of breathing in and breathing out. True spirituality is not a removal from the world, but it is discovering the capacity of our hearts to open and awaken in the midst of all the circumstances of life.

In a recent gathering of Buddhist teachers that I attended, the Dalai Llama said, "It doesn't matter to me if there's one more Buddhist in the world. What matters is that we all learn to treat each other with respect and kindness." If that is possible, it will transform human life, and that's the essence of what he offers. Many people have seen spirituality as a vehicle to run away from their problems, but the problems almost always follow them. Even in the monasteries where I've lived, people would try to run away from their problems, but they'd realize while sitting quietly in a forest or a cave that the problems would be there with them. Wherever you go, there you are.

We live in a society where we've attained Olympic levels of distraction. There are so many ways that we can distract ourselves from our lives and from the problems of our lives. How do we deal with all the distractions?

We've been called by some an addicted society. Perhaps you are right to say that we are a distracted society. We're being sold that distraction by media and by school systems, which in some ways benefit from our unconsciousness. We consume more, we ignore racism, and we ignore the pollution of the environment if we are busy with distractions. Part of the genuine task of spiritual life, and it's a very heartfelt one, is to regain a respect for life. And for most Westerners, that respect comes from slowing down. It's not a removal from life, but a willingness to turn off the TV sometimes, a willingness to walk in nature, to pray or meditate, or just to spend more time with our children in an authentic way. The things that are meaningful appear when we turn away from those distractions.

Most people who come to the meditation retreats that I've taught for years find the first few days terribly difficult. It's like a rushing stream that all of a sudden empties into a big lake, and all the sediment and silt drops out. After a few days, however, they find it wonderful just to be undistracted and able to pay attention when they drink a cup of tea. So there's an art to it that we can relearn. And the teachings of meditation and prayer around the world give us the vehicle for learning how to be undistracted and truly connected with ourselves.

When we accomplish that solitude, how do we bring that feeling that comes with the solitude and the silence back into our busy lives?

The first answer is that it's not easy. Any guru or system that tells you, "There is a very simple way you can do it; just send your money and we will teach you," is probably a waste of your money. This is the central spiritual task of our culture. We've lost our sense of the sacred, and to recover it is like swimming upstream, but there are several things that can help. The first is to get a clear sense of the true direction of spirituality. The true awakening lies in discovering a greater capacity for love, compassion, and balance.

In the Buddhist tradition, there is a teaching called "the near enemies of awakening." Accepting these near enemies as truth prevents us from realizing our spiritual potential. For example, the near enemy of love is attachment. When we love someone, we want them to be the way they are, but when the relationship turns into attachment, then there is a grasping quality. The other person seems different, separate, and we want to possess them.

Similarly, the near enemy of compassion is pity. "Oh, that poor person is suffering," we say, but do not really involve ourselves. Whereas true compassion is the shared heart of our joys and our sorrows. The near enemy of balance, or spiritual equanimity, is indifference. It masquerades as spirituality. We say, "It doesn't matter. Easy come, easy go. This marriage isn't working out; I'll try another. I could have more children." Indifference masks our fear of revealing ourselves and making ourselves vulnerable.

We must be aware of these near enemies to avoid them and realize our potential. The awakened spiritual potential is an opening of the heart and the mind in the midst of all things. It's not motivated by fear but rather by discovery, recognizing the great heart of the Buddha that we each contain. It is a great human

capacity for presence and freedom of spirit in the midst of any cir-
cumstance. That's why we revere the greatest sages and teachers.
Not because they left the world, but because they lived in the
midst of it with such great love and freedom.

Perhaps the near enemy of the spiritual would be something
that permeates our society, and that is cynicism. Can you carry
that to the rational, the reasonable, as well.

It's a view of the world that feels true, and yet it forgets the
grace, the mystery, and also the difficulty of what it means to really love another person. I've spent some time doing hospice work,
particularly with people who are dying of AIDS. And at the end of
life, when one has lived a life with some consciousness, one looks
back, and the questions are so simple and basic: Did I live fully,
and did I love well? I think these are questions we all ask ourselves. To make sure we get the answer we want, we need to ask
ourselves early on how to accomplish these tasks.

Suppose we have a tight schedule and three kids that we need
to get to the school bus in the morning. How do we manage it?
First, we need to understand that where we are is our practice.
Getting the kids on the school bus is as much a spiritual discipline
as going to the Buddha hall and chanting on a cold morning or
doing some ascetic practice in a Christian monastery. In some
ways, it's harder, because when your guru or the abbot says get up
and pray all night, you might be sleepy and roll over, but when
your children are crying and sick in bed, you get up, you serve, and
you offer your love and comfort. So the path that we've chosen is
a difficult one, but it is also filled with the potential for a great
awakening of compassion and wisdom.

When you go into a Zen monastery, you learn how to hold a
cup of tea, how to hold a bowl of food, or how to fold your robes.

And it is in these details that you begin to feel the spirit of awakening. It's not some great insight. Rather, it is how that awakening is translated through the cells of your body.

What happens in spiritual practice, then, is a shift of identity. There is a wonderful story about Pope John the 23rd that exemplifies this. He is said to have written that "Sometimes I would think about a difficult problem at night half awake, try to solve it, and then realize that I would have to speak to the Pope about it. Then I would awaken more fully and remember, *I am the Pope!*"

Spiritual practice requires us to ask at some point: *Who am I to have been born into this body, and what is my task here? What is the purpose of this life?* And when we ask those questions of ourselves, then they begin to inform all that we do. Our purpose clearly does not lie in having possessions, because we cannot keep them. We are just passing through. Purpose is derived from learning to love and in remembering who we are.

When a young man from south-central L.A. was told he had his whole life ahead of him, his response was, "Kids in my neighborhood are dying at 18, 19, and 20." How does your message apply to a young person who lives in the ghetto and feels that he or she has no future?

That's a difficult and agonizing issue. I recently heard the statistic that nearly 40 percent of young African-American men between the ages of 15 and 25 are either in prison or on parole. More than any society but South Africa—and perhaps for some of the same reasons—we have issues of racism that we still have not addressed.

I recently had the privilege of being part of a retreat with Michael Meade, a wonderful mythologist; Malidoma Somé, an African medicine man; and Louis Rodriguez, a Latino poet who works with gangs in Los Angeles. The retreat was called "The Absence of Elders in the Violence of Youth." For a week, 100 men, including many young men from the ghetto, considered the issue of the violence of young men. The young men were very angry, and partly they were angry because they had no sense of future. Partly, they were angry because they felt that no one knew who they were. There was no older man to hear their story, to see their beauty, to feel their pain.

The first few days of the retreat, we just listened, and they talked. Basically, they said, "You can't do this. Do you know what a terrible world we've inherited from you?" But their language was a lot stronger than that. They simply wanted to be heard and respected and met. Sometimes they'd sit in the back with their arms folded, looking nonchalant, as if they really didn't care what was being said. But we found that even though they didn't look as if they were listening, they were. There were Vietnam veterans who stood up and told stories of their time in Vietnam. There were men who had been in prison who stood up and told their stories. The young men heard things that they needed to hear from their elders, and that made it possible for them to envision life and transformation.

One of the key elements in all of spiritual life is making ourselves available to others. What young men need is initiation, someone to whom they can show their stuff and really prove it— otherwise, they do it in the street. They need respect. Without it, the pain becomes so great that despair takes over. And it is manifested in the drug trade, in crime, and sometimes in burning down their own house because that's the only way to get someone to notice them. I see that as grief, as an expression of pain.

Part of that retreat, the end of it, involved going back into Watts and planting four trees. We wanted to create a grove where the elders of the community could sit on this bench—like an African traditional elders' bench—and young men could come and tell their stories and be listened to and listen to the elders. But when we got back after a week together, we learned that one of the young men in the group had just died in a drive-by shooting. So instead of the celebration we'd planned, we drummed and chanted a lament for the unnecessary violence and suffering that men have inflicted upon one another for so long. By grieving and lamenting, we could sit together and say, "We pledge our hearts to respect one another, to heal this."

The meditation or the work we do in the inner city must contain the underlying principle of respect. We must shape our vision of life by really listening from our heart rather than from our ambition. And that transformation—whether we go on retreat, pray, or walk in nature—is what allows us to come back to the office or to come back to our life and offer something beautiful.

Isn't there also the idea that the death of the young man affects us, that somehow we are connected to him in a mysterious way? Isn't the grief over his death representative of our grief and lament over every death?

That's right. There were so many tears that came at that time because we were open and connected, and we knew that. My teacher in Asia said that to undertake a spiritual life is simply to stop making war—making war with what's too big and what's too small and what's right and what's wrong. We need to stop trying to fight all the time. The first step of spiritual life is just to stop, not to run away, but to look, to listen, and to be open. When we look at the world, then we see that there is an enormous amount of greed, hatred, prejudice, and racism. That's one of the first facts that we face. And there is suffering in the world. The question is, What do we do with that suffering? Is there redemption? Is there value in that suffering?

The fact is that the world doesn't need more oil, and it doesn't need more food. There's enough food to feed everyone already. There are grain elevators full of food, and there are people starving in other countries. The world needs less greed, less fear, less prejudice, and less hatred. Those forces are in the human heart. So it becomes a great political act, a transformative act, to find some vehicle to face our own fear, our own hatred, our own racism and prejudice. Then it becomes possible in our actions to really transform the society around us.

Joanna Macy, who is a wonderful teacher and good friend, recently returned from Russia where she was teaching her nuclear empowerment work on despair. Actually, she was in the Ukraine near Chernobyl, in the closest inhabited city to the Chernobyl nuclear plant. Almost everyone left that area after the accident. They are now back, but they live in their houses and apartments with the windows sealed, and they can't go outside. There are beautiful mountains and forests. They have pictures of the forests on the wall. And when she asked about all of this, they got angry with her.

"How dare you come and rub our noses in the pain of this," they said. Finally, one man stood up and said, "She comes and we speak about it so we can tell our children at least that we faced it." Someone else said, "Well, how long before we can go into our forests?" And the mayor said, "Not in my great grandchildren's lifetime, and not in their great grandchildren's lifetime." And another woman stood up and said, "We speak about it so that Joanna and others can go back and warn the world not to let this happen to other children."

Our capacity to transform the sorrows of the world through our compassion is the heart of spiritual practice. What we are asked to do is not run away, but to discover that we can breathe in and out, that we can rest in our human bodies, that we can let our tears fall, and that we can listen to one another with the respect of a Buddha.

In some ways, our high-tech toys and our televisions have deadened us to life's pain and suffering. We look at these pictures of children in Bosnia or wherever, and we see the suffering, but it sort of goes through us. It's almost unreal because it's so tragic and awful, and we shut ourselves off from it. The United States is one of the more insulated nations in the world. We think that everybody has the same blessings we have, and it's really not true. At the same time, we are surrounded by these distractions that deaden us even when we see the pictures of what's going on around the world. Somehow we don't get it, and that has to change.

There is always a wake-up call. Sometimes it takes the form of your partner coming home and saying, "I went to the doctor today, and she said I have a tumor." Or sometimes it happens when someone that you love dearly has died, or the business that you put all your love and energy into fails. All of a sudden, you are thrown back on yourself. Society tries to insulate us. It's like the Buddha being insulated in these beautiful palaces, with his father trying to protect him from the world, but one day he saw a dead body. And he said, "Who does this happen to?" The charioteer said, "It happens to everyone." That stopped him in his tracks. That blow comes to us all, and although it's terrible, it is also a gift, because it reminds us what we are here for, and really what it means to be a human being.

We need to get in touch with our compassion and lovingkindness, and there are traditional ways to cultivate it or practice it from the Buddhist perspective. This opens us to a sense of wonder in the world that in some ways we know so little about. Where did the earth come from? What is consciousness? What is love? It is vital to our self-awareness that we ask these deep questions.

There is a beautiful book called *Children's Letters to God* that I like to read at times. The book consists of one-sentence, handwritten letters by children. Here are a few of them: *Dear God, Are you really invisible or is that just a trick? Lucy. Dear God, Instead of letting people die and having to make new ones, why don't you just keep the ones you've got now? Dear God, Did you mean for the giraffe to look like that, or was it an accident? Nan.*

I read these letters and realize that as adults, we lose that sense of wonder and innocent curiosity. It's almost as if we look at but do not see the sunset, the stars, human life. Where is our sense of wonder about the fact that we breathe, the fact that a human being is born out of the body of a woman? Or that we have a hole at one end of our body into which we stuff dead plants and animals and grind them up with these little bones, and it nourishes us? Is that who we are? This physical body? We seem to lose that ability to wonder, and then something awakens us. And if we have the support, the resources, and the understanding we need, then this awakening starts to sweep our life in a whole new direction.

Can this awakening—the kind of transformation that you are talking about—take place without trauma?

The Buddha said there are four ways that spiritual practice proceeds: Quickly and with no pain (with pleasure); slowly and with pleasure; quickly but with great suffering; and for most people, slowly and with suffering. I wish I could say that for most people suffering wasn't a part of their path, but in some way, I think we need it. You can't separate joy and sorrow. They are in the same breath—like birth and death. We have this illusion that we'll make the world perfect, clean, and modern, and there will be no pollution and no bacteria. But that's not life. Life is messy and bloody and beautiful and sorrowful—all in the same breath.

Are you saying that it is important for us to welcome suffering, embrace suffering? That sounds kind of hopeless. Where do we find hope in the midst of having to embrace suffering?

We can learn from the words of Martin Luther King, Jr., right after his church was bombed. People were in great despair, and he encouraged them in this way:

> We will match your capacity to inflict suffering with our capacity to endure suffering. We will meet your physical force with soul force. We will not hate you, but we cannot in good conscience obey your unjust laws. We will soon wear you down with our capacity to suffer. And in winning our freedom, we will so appeal to your heart that we will win yours as well.

There are two great forces in the world: Those who are unafraid to kill, and those who are unafraid to die. Those who are unafraid to kill govern a lot of countries by means of guns and armaments. The only thing that equals that force are those who are not afraid to die. We need to be among those who are not afraid. Our capacity to open to life is what gives our heart courage, is what gives us, in some way, meaning. It is actually through despair that we transform the world and make it a place of compassion.

In Buddhist tradition, there are specific practices used to transform the sufferings of the world and to develop the spirit of lovingkindness in daily life. I use these practices in traffic jams, while waiting in lines, waiting for appointments, and so forth. The basic principle consists of reminding ourselves about what we already know through visualization, repetition, and certain traditional phrases that begin with forgiveness.

Forgiveness itself is often confusing to people. They believe that to forgive means somehow that you forget, and then whatever injustice happened will happen over again. Forgiveness is, in fact, one of the most important acts of human life because it is the way that we let go of the past. Without forgiveness, situations such as those in Serbia, Croatia, and Bosnia happen over and over again. There is an endless chain of recrimination—they did this to me, I will do this to them—and there is no possibility of freedom. So one of the central acts of spiritual life lies in practicing forgiveness and learning to let go.

What forgiveness means to the heart is a kind of healing that does not condone the past. For example, one might say, "I will forgive this, but I will never allow it to happen again. I will put my body in the way of allowing it to happen again." This kind of affirmation doesn't say that what happened is okay, and it doesn't mean that you even have to relate to the offending person. You may forgive someone and say, "I want nothing more to do with him or her." What it does mean is that an inner act of release takes place; we let go of resentment and hatred and stop perpetuating it in the world. At a fundamental level, this release greatly benefits us.

The practice of forgiveness is often a process that includes working through grief, anger, rage, and sorrow. But by using the traditional practices—or whatever way one works with forgiveness—we learn to recognize that the pain we all carry, that we've all shared, is too great to turn into hatred. For example, when I was in India with my wife some years ago, her brother died of suicide. She had a vision of death the day that we were on a mountaintop at an ashram. She came and told me about it, and I said, "Oh, it's just part of the meditation process of letting go."

A week later we received a telegram saying that her brother had died, and it was dated on the same day as his death and in the way that she'd seen. She was halfway around the world, how could she know? But she did, and it is because we are interconnected. To forgive or to develop compassion has an effect on every other being in the world. It doesn't mean it transforms them. That's their own path. But it has an effect, and you know it immediately. Longfellow wrote, "If we could read the secret history of our enemies, we should find in each person's life sorrow and suffering enough to disarm all hostility."

In practicing forgiveness meditations, we must begin with ourselves. We need to look at our lives and feel the places where we've been hurt or harmed ourselves out of our own fear, confusion, pain, or anger. While picturing the hurt, and sensing it, we must extend mercy to ourselves and say, "I did the best I could at that time. I offer myself forgiveness." We need to repeat that a number of times.

In a similar way, we can picture those who have been harmed or hurt by us. We must remember the sorrows that we carry from that experience, and in remembering, we ask, "May I be forgiven?" Often what people feel at first is, "No, I can't." So part of the practice is really learning to weep or to grieve or to be angry; we need to feel all of those emotions and to touch all of them with mercy. We need to ask, "Can I hold my own human life with mercy, with kindness?"

Finally, the most difficult part lies in forgiving those who have hurt us. We need to feel that hurt in our bodies, to remember the images. And then, when we are ready, we can say, "I release you. I forgive you for the past, and I let go of the hatred that I carry." When I was given this practice in the monastery, my teacher said, "Do this practice several times a day for the next six months to a year, and then we'll talk about it." So we need to do this practice a lot. We can't do it in just one sitting. But gradually we can sense it as a direction of the heart.

There's a parallel practice that we can also do, and that is the cultivation of the heart of lovingkindness. The basis of this is the recognition that what we all most deeply long for is to be loved, to be honored. We search for it in many guises. There is the story of two young children—a six-year-old boy and his eight-year-old sister. She had a rare blood disease and was going to die if she didn't find a blood donor. They searched for donors, but it turned out that the only compatible blood donor was her six-year-old brother. So he was asked by the mother and doctor if he would donate his blood to save his sister's life? And he said, "I have to think about it." Six-year-olds are actually very thoughtful if you know young children. After a couple of days, he came back and said, "All right, I'll do it." So they went to the doctor's office, and the children lay down side by side. Blood was taken from the boy and given to his sister as he watched. When he could see that she was feeling stronger from it, he called the doctor over and said, "Will I start to die right away?" He hadn't understood that giving his blood for her life wouldn't mean taking his own—which is why he had to think about it for a few days.

I believe we all have that place in us where we recognize our connection to one another. This connection is what enables us to risk ourselves for others. So another great force in the world that counters the power of arms is the power of lovingkindness. It explains how Gandhi can go to east Pakistan at the time they send 60,000 troops to west Pakistan, and Gandhi is more effective through his soul force than the 60,000 armed soldiers. Let me give one more example, and then discuss the teachings of lovingkindness.

I had the privilege of working in the Cambodian refugee camps some years ago with a wonderful monk, an elder who survived the holocaust in Cambodia. He decided to build a temple in the Khmer Rouge camp of 50,000 people. These people had watched their villages destroyed and their loved ones killed—not a single family had remained intact. So we built this bamboo temple and invited people to come. But the Khmer Rouge underground in the camps threatened to kill anyone who went to this temple. We didn't know who would come, but he rang the gong after the temple was built, and 20,000 people came to the square and sat as he began the ancient chanting. They hadn't heard this sound throughout the war, and people just sat in a kind of stunned silence as he chanted.

And then it was time for him to speak. What could he say to people who had been through such destruction and loss? Ghosananda, this monk, took one of the first passages from the Buddha, and he chanted in Sanskrit and English the words, "Hatred never ends by hatred, but by love alone is healed. This is the ancient and eternal law." He chanted this over and over, and people started to chant with him, and they wept—they wept for their own sorrow and out of the realization that the truth he spoke was even greater than their suffering.

The practice of lovingkindness generally begins with one's self. You can practice while sitting quietly at home with your eyes closed, in the middle of a traffic jam in your car, or in the doctor's waiting room. You feel your own breath and life, and with each breath you feel how you treasure your life. Think about what you would do to care for yourself. And after that, think of the image from the Buddha of a mother or father holding their beloved child. Perhaps you hold yourself as a child in your mind, and you recite inwardly the phrases, "May I be well. May I be filled with lovingkindness. May my heart be at peace." Recite those over and over until you feel that mercy and kindness for yourself.

Then, you might say, "I'm aware of the sorrows that I carry, and I hold those with compassion. May I be filled with compassion." Feeling that for one's self is quite difficult for some people. After you do that, then gradually extend the feeling to someone you love a lot, and say, "May they be well. May they be filled with lovingkindness." Then, extend the feeling to include the people around you, and finally to the whole the world. Or you can focus on the people who are causing difficulty for you or others.

If you work with this meditation, you can walk down the street and, without looking strange, you can do a blessing for each person who passes. As a person walks by, say, "May you be well, may you be happy, and may your heart be filled with lovingkindness." Or offer your blessing to the person sitting next to you in the airplane. All of a sudden, instead of the isolation we mentioned, after five minutes of inwardly reciting the well-being of others to yourself and those around you, you feel a sense of communion. When you get off the airplane and pick up your baggage, you could almost wave good-bye to everybody because you've made that moment's heart connection. These are some of the traditional practices, and they speak of how to cultivate forgiveness and lovingkindness in the midst of life rather than removed from life.

You're saying that in the process of embracing lovingkindness, we can heal ourselves?

The healing of ourselves is the same as the healing of the world. We must face the pain that we carry and stop running away or distracting ourselves. Then, we can take the seat that the Buddha took—or any other great sage—and say, "I will run no longer. I will open my eyes and ears and heart to the whole catastrophe of life, its beauty and sorrows." When we can heal the things that we run from, we can bring the gift of our heart to politics, economics, education, farming, the land—all the things that so need it.

As we learn how to practice lovingkindness and forgiveness and are compassionate with ourselves and become compassionate with others, there is a process of change and transformation that goes on, and we move toward maturity. Can you describe that process?

Initially and beautifully, for people in spiritual life there's a kind of idealistic phase, a romance, a honeymoon, that we pass through, whether it's with a guru or lama or whether it's with Jesus or Mary, it doesn't matter. In this phase, we hope that everything in the world will be changed by our spirit and by their light, and it is, but often not in the way that we expect. The change isn't so much in the world, but it's a change in the heart and a change in consciousness. As we mature, we shift away from that idealism of trying to perfect the world, perfect the diet, and perfect states of mind. Meditation is actually very humbling. The mind has very little pride, and it will do almost anything. We discover that it's not about that kind of perfection, but rather it's about the perfection of our kindness, the perfection of our freedom in the midst of things, and the perfection of mercy.

That shift in attitude requires or asks of us several different qualities. Rather than idealism, we must cultivate a kind of patience, or another beautiful word for it is a quality of *grace*. The Tao tells us that spring comes, and the grass grows by itself. You can't hurry up spiritual process or human life. And where are we going? The only place we are really going is where we are—*here*. There is no other place. So instead of trying to accomplish or change things, it's more a matter of resting with the moment, with a graciousness and an ease, like music with some harmony—even with the difficulties and sorrows. As one great Zen master wrote, "To be enlightened is to be without anxiety about nonperfection."

The world isn't perfect the way we'd like it to be. It never was, and it never will be. To be awakened is not to struggle but to serve in some way. Answers are not black and white. Every life has every facet to it. For example, a friend of mine did a training session for the U.S. Army Green Berets. He worked with them on meditation, body work, and so forth. Many of his friends were so upset, they wouldn't talk to him while he did it. I think it was a wonderful thing to do. He held a month-long retreat for the Green Berets. These are guys who have been in combat and do night parachute jumps from high altitudes into the ocean, but they said sitting still for a month in retreat was the most difficult thing they had ever done. My friend told me, "I saw these guys sitting there in this camp out in the woods in meditation, with their rifles, their M16s next to them. They wore T-shirts that said '82nd Airborne Division, Death from Above,' with a bomber or something on them. I looked at them and wondered what I was accomplishing." Yet, this is a perfect image because the world is filled with Bosnias, and we can't avert our gaze—we need to respond to it. Spiritual maturity is really about growing the capacity of our own heart to breathe in the sorrows of the world and breathe out our kindness, to make our deeds speak our values, and to integrate that without judgment, without idealism. We must learn to live what we believe.

It's also important to remember that the heart is like a flower. It's not as if we are going to remain open and loving all the time. Sometimes when it's cold at night, the flower closes, and it needs to—that's part of our humanity. To embrace our humanity means that we love ourselves as we are, as well as loving and accepting others. That's what the world needs.

It's often said that the sorrows of one who awakens increase, but the capacity for love and compassion also increases, so that we are able to transform. Like art or poetry or music, we take the world, and we make it into something. It really is an offering of the sacred.

Buckminster Fuller once said, "As we develop the capacity to solve problems, our problems just get bigger." Of course our opportunities are bigger, too. So there's the compassion and kindness and loving side of it. You never know where you're going to find wisdom.

The earth is our mother. Whatever befalls the earth, befalls the sons and daughters of the earth. All things are connected—just as the blood unites a family. William Blake put it in another way. He said, "If one is to do good, it must be done in the minute particulars. General good is the plea of the hypocrite, the flatterer, and the scoundrel." Our focus is not on the ideals, but on the details of daily existence. How do we drive? What do we do with our money? When we hold our money, do we see sacred images on it and realize it's energy? When we hand it to someone, what is the quality of attention that we bring to that act? In the midst of our life, we can awaken.

❖❖❖

EPILOGUE

Numerous practical insights come through here, not the least of which is the emphasis Kornfield places on the importance of forgiveness. It is so crucial that we forgive ourselves and not carry the guilt. As we are able to heal ourselves, so also will the world be healed. Shifting our attitude and developing patience allows us to experience the beauty of grace. We begin to appreciate the natural flow of life—that where we are going is where we are—here and now in the moment. What the world needs more than change is love, that we truly embrace our humanity, loving ourselves as we are, and loving and accepting others as well. The journey of life is a moment-to-moment process, and each detail and act presents an opportunity to awaken.

❖❖❖ ❖❖❖

CHAPTER EIGHT

Schlepping Toward Enlightenment

Lama Surya Das
and Michael Toms

PROLOGUE

*W*e are fortunate to live in a time when so many of the world's great religious teachings are available to us. Not the least of these are the teachings that have emerged from the one-time-hidden mountain villages of Tibet. Perhaps paramount among these great Tibetan spiritual teachings is what is known as the consummate vehicle, "Dzogchen," which in a profound way is not Buddhist—or even a philosophy or a religion—nor is it a transcendent reality. Rather, it is simply a direct seeing of the true primordial nature of being. This is the focus of the following discussion with Lama Surya Das.

Lama Surya Das is an American poet and storyteller. He is the author of The Snow Lion's Turquoise Mane: Wisdom Tales from Tibet, co-author of The Natural Great Perfection: Spontaneous Songs and Dzogchen Teachings, and Awakening the Buddha

Within: Eight Steps to Enlightenment. *Surya Das is a Buddhist scholar, meditation teacher, a lama of the Nyingma order, a translator of Tibetan tales, and a specialist in oriental religions and poetry. He spent ten years in the Himalayas and a year in Kyoto, Japan; and Korea. He has led many groups to monasteries and on mountain pilgrimages to Nepal, India, and Tibet, and he has studied with Buddhist teachers of all schools for more than 25 years. He has twice completed the traditional three-year, three-month Vajrayana retreat. He is the founder of the Dzogchen Foundation of America, based in Cambridge, Massachusetts; and he leads meditation workshops, seminars, and spiritual retreats worldwide.*

❖❖❖

MICHAEL TOMS: *When you got out of college, what led you to find Tibetan teachings? How did that happen for you?*

LAMA SURYA DAS: Something called, and I semiconsciously heard it and followed and listened. In fact, it was more subtle than I was, so I really didn't know what it was consciously at that time. During college in the sixties, I'd been involved a bit in seeking, as many of us were in various ways. I had done Zen and some chanting, and I had met Ram Dass and been to encounter groups and gestalt workshops. I went to Esalen to see what was there and enjoyed the hot tubs, but I couldn't stay in them forever. One thing led to another. I felt a pull, and I kept going east, to Europe, the Middle East, and India. In India, I found myself with different saints and teachers, and one thing led to another. I am Jewish on my parents' side, but some lamas have told me that I seem to have Buddhist blood from past lives.

My first guru was Neem Karoli Baba—Ram Dass's teacher— and he gave me the name Surya Das, which means "a servant of the light" or "a disciple of the sun." He was a wonderful teacher; he embodied unconditional love. He sensed his kinship with all, and that was a very heart-opening message for me. Like many male Western intellectuals, I was just living from the eyebrows up—very cerebral—and I interpreted my Buddhist meditation in a way that helped me be even more cerebral at that time. But with Maharaj-ji, or Neem Karoli Baba, there was a balance of head and heart. This great master really embodied service to God through serving others. He really helped round out my spiritual life and especially struck a chord of devotion that I later found most enriching. That devotion and heartfelt means of bringing devotion and love to others and to higher principles has really sustained me since then.

There is some misunderstanding about the concept of devotion, particularly as it relates to teachers and gurus. The term spiritual tyranny *has emerged in American culture, which refers to those people who have been taken over by teachers who have, perhaps, fallen from the path. Can you talk about that from your perspective?*

We can be taken over by powerful teachers or leaders if we give ourselves away. Why do we do that? That's something I look into in myself. Why do we disempower ourselves and make ourselves helpless so that we feel victimized? This is not to say there have not been spiritual tyrants or some exploitation and abuse of power on the part of charismatic leaders of all kinds. The Aum Shinri Kyo cult in Tokyo is a good example of this. Shoko Asahara, the leader, called himself a Buddhist teacher, and he asserted that killing was in the name of truth. This is not Buddhism, this is not dharma, this is not even sanity. We need to make sure that when we devote ourselves to a cause, it is not just to an individual—no matter how charismatic—but to the higher principles upon which a cause is built.

My devotion has been to truth, sanity, love, connection, friends, family, and the greater family of all beings—not just human beings. The teacher must embody a principle. The guru is like a door to God, truth, and our higher nature, and we don't have to get stuck in the door frame. We can go through the door into the mansion of the highest truth. We don't have to give ourselves away. Of course, we can talk in other terms about surrender, about letting ourselves go, but I think there must be a balance between healthy individuation and that kind of merging with others for a cause.

In the United States, we place an emphasis on the individual and being an individual. In some ways, this is the very essence of being an American. Those of us who are born here in the United States seem to carry that trait in our genes, in our bones. How do we balance that with the sense of opening ourselves to a larger reality?

We need to realize that our concept of individualism is compatible with the idea of surrender to a higher principle. I think Jack Engler, a Vipassana teacher and psychiatrist, once said, "We have to have a healthy ego, a grown-up mature ego, an adult ego, before we can transcend the ego. Otherwise, we are like people who never grow up. We become dependent, and we stay dependent our whole lives." We must first cultivate a healthy ego, and then transcend the ego to become one with the universe and really serve others as ourselves. It is part of the developmental process from infancy into maturity and then into transcendence. Those are general developmental principles.

Neem Karoli Baba was Indian, and his teachings essentially came out of the Hindu tradition. What was the bridge that got you into the Buddhist tradition?

I went around in those days saying, "Teach me what you know." What did I know of mantras? I'm a Jewish boy from Long Island. My mantra was "Teach me what you know." I wanted information from everyone: Sufis in Turkey, gestalt teachers, poets and artists, philosophers, and college mentors. And I wasn't really thinking about becoming a Buddhist. In fact, these days, when I speak to others, I ask: "Why become a Buddhist when you can become a Buddha?" That's bigger than Buddhism. We are all Buddhas by nature, so it is incumbent upon us, I think, to become all that we are. So, as did many of my fellow travelers on the path—seekers all—I went from ashram to ashram, from monastery to monastery, from retreat to retreat, from pilgrimage to pilgrimage, and teacher to teacher, learning from whomever I could, learning from the fools as well as the wise.

I ended up mostly with Tibetan lamas, but I also spent a lot of time with Hindu masters such as Neem Karoli Baba and Muktananda and the great female saint of India, AnandamayiMa. I studied in Burma, did some retreats there, and I lived a year in Japan studying Zen. I've always been involved with Zen because I love Chinese poetry and Japanese haiku. The Zen aesthetics and the Zen stories always inspire me. So I feel like an American Buddhist, and I feel that I'm thinking more like a Boddhisattva— trying to live an impeccable, enlightened life for the benefit of all.

Do you think there is an American Buddhism that is taking shape?

There is a sort of emergent American Buddhism taking shape, and we can see some trends already that distinguish it. As Buddhism has moved from country to country, it has been assimilated into a culture. The essence of Buddhism, or the luminous heart of the dharma, remains the same, but the form it takes changes with time and place. So in America, we see four or five main characteristics emerging. One characteristic of American Buddhism, for example, is that it's more democratic—not so hierarchical. There is also room for women, not just as equals but as teachers. There is also much emphasis on practice, not theory and dogma, but meditation practice. And it is psychologically astute, relating more to therapy, philosophy, and science than depending on theology, cosmology, and beliefs.

We can also say of American Buddhism that it is "essentialized" rather than ritualized. It's also nonsectarian; this is the first time in history that all the extant schools of Buddhism exist in the same place, side by side. Once again, America acts as a melting pot. We all have to get along; we have to understand and respect each other and love each other. Nobody has a corner on the market of truth.

Buddhism and Buddhist teachings seem to be eminently practical; it is in some ways a very commonsense approach to life. What is your perspective on that?

I think common sense is wisdom, and we don't need to mystify wisdom. If it doesn't show up in life as common sense, as sagacity, as sanity, what good is it? Buddhism *is* a very practical tradition. It's called "a way of life." It's not called a religion, because it doesn't discuss the creator and so on. As I indicate in my book *Awakening the Buddha Within: Eight Steps to Enlightenment,* Buddhism is about principles of enlightened living. It's about practices for daily life—not just meditating on a mountaintop. There are practices such as right livelihood, or, as I call it, impeccable vocation. This is part of the eight steps to enlightenment—the eightfold path. There's also impeccable speech, right exercise, and right eating. These are all parts of the eightfold path in a modern redaction.

We need enlightenment in every aspect of our lives, not just up in the rarefied atmosphere somewhere. If it's an authentic enlightenment, it's true freedom. If it's a spiritual path, it's a spiritual life—not just spiritual on Sundays. And it's not just spiritual in the temple, synagogue, church, or mosque. God is everywhere, if we want to speak in that language, and has to appear everywhere. In my teachings and in my practice, I particularly emphasize bringing the dharma home. When that happens, we can live a sane life, an honest life, loving the cats and the mice, and not just praying for all beings to be enlightened in the great perfection—which is a wonderful prayer with a huge scope, but it's also very abstract. We don't want to pray like that and then be kicking the cats and killing the mice and swatting the mosquitoes.

We must try to bring the dharma down to a very practical level. Do we really see the Buddha and the light in each person we relate to, or do we just think of the Buddha as a faraway light in heaven—or on the so-called other shore of nirvana. I think living in the present has a lot to do with it. If we are really present, everything is available in the present. This is not a new idea. All the mystics say this, but it's also fresh every moment. Everything is available within the natural state, within this very present moment, and within pure presence. So it's very practical to just be present. Even to meditate sounds a little special. We can cultivate wakefulness and mindfulness through meditating and other contemplative disciplines, but it all converges in the present—it's now or never, as always. And the more present we are, the more it—whatever we seek—is here, and is us. Because we are what we seek, what we seek we are. It is here or nowhere. The problem is, we are always elsewhere. It's always right here. And presence provides access to that.

We can cultivate presence with centering practices, including meditation, and also formless practices such as doing our work in a mindful or sacred manner, relating in a sacred manner, not just venerating teachers, but venerating everyone. It's actually a Vajrayana Tibetan practice called Pure Perceptions, or Sacred Outlook, recognizing the Buddha in everyone. Then we can begin to treat everyone as we would like to be treated. We need to recognize the light in everyone and everything, for it is shining in everyone and everything.

We are talking about the emergence of Buddhism in the Western form, and that just brings to mind the Judeo-Christian tradition, which in some sense has been oriented toward externals. Christian tradition reflects the idea that if we suffer in this life, we'll get to heaven. It also includes the idea of original sin. The Jewish tradition embraces the idea of the Messiah coming—something coming—from the external. Yet in Buddhism, we have this idea of original nature, which is a different view from that of original sin. Do you think the differences between the traditions may be a motivational attraction for Westerners?

In Buddhism, the idea of original good nature is very different from the idea of original sin. Buddhism embraces the idea that we are all Buddhas by nature and contain the original goodness of Buddha. All we have to do is awaken to that and to recognize that. Of course, if we look into the mystic traditions of the theistic religions such as Christianity, Judaism, and Islam, a similar belief exists; there is the notion that the highest good is there—God is within each of us. But we've lost touch with that today, so people have turned to the East to recover that way of thinking. There's a lot of Christian and Jewish mysticism that is very similar to the perennial philosophies of the East, and I can read it between the lines in the Bible and the Torah and so on. I think that this bridge between East and West is a very harmonizing influence today. In fact, I rediscovered Judaism and Christianity through my Buddhist and Eastern yoga experience. As I get older, I feel more and more Jewish, and I recognize how much being Jewish and a New Yorker is part of my family lineage—but I am also part of all human lineage. And Buddhism connects me to that.

Christians and Jews place more emphasis on the future; they believe that Jesus—or the Messiah—is coming. A Buddhist believes that Buddha is here, now. And this is the good news of Buddhism: that it is now. Buddha is within each of us. It is only a matter of awakening to that, or awakening the Buddha within and being all that we are and can be. It is not as far away as it seems. We are not waiting for the Messiah or for the next Buddha. We can find it in ourselves. As Rabbi Hillel said in the second century, "If not you, who? And if not now, when?" He was a rabbi, but this is Bodhisattva talk. This is Buddhist. This is dharma talk. The Messiah is the anointed one within. It is up to us to discover that now, not to wait until after we're dead to be reborn somewhere in heaven or in the pure lands.

This is the genius of dharma Buddhism that really speaks to us today. It is very present; it is profound yet simple. That doesn't necessarily mean it's easy, but it is simple. And it's workable, doable—each of us can do it. In fact, the Buddha said, "Be a lamp unto yourself. I, the teacher, just point the way." In a way, to use modern terms, this is the ultimate self-help manual. It's do-it-yourself enlightenment, freedom, and nirvanic peace. This is not waiting for something else to happen or someone else to do it for you. Of course, teachers and teachings can help facilitate enlightenment, but we still have to pick up our sick beds and our victimized pose and walk.

In some of the Buddhist seminars and retreats, there is still this idea that somehow it would be almost impossible to really be a

Buddha in this life. One would have to live a perfect life, and that can't be done. How would you respond to that?

It's not easy. It can be harder or more subtle than we think. On the one hand, it's very special and a huge spiritual mountain to climb. Tibet has preserved these teachings intact for 2,000 years in a cloistered, pure environment. There are a few living masters today, and there are living Buddhas. The Dalai Lama, for example, is a remarkable individual, and he is the humblest person in the world. On the other hand, it's not just that there are enlightened people. There is enlightened activity. There are enlightened moments. We can all participate in that. It is not that far from us. The Tantric teachings promise that we can achieve full Buddhahood in this lifetime. According to Dzogchen teachings, if we practice assiduously, it can happen in as few as three years. So it is not as far away as we might think. Even if we feel far from it, we need to remember that it is never far from us.

You have a wonderful story about your experience with some children in Austin, Texas, that illustrates how we have to relearn what we've forgotten. Would you relate that story?

I had given a weekend retreat, and on Monday, I was invited to the Montessori school. I love children, but we don't see that many children at dharma centers because there is so much emphasis on meditation and philosophy. I met for an hour with a class of nine-year-olds. I sat sort of at the head of the room on the floor. I had a little gong and a little cushion, but nothing very formal. When the kids came into the room, rather than sitting down like an audience, they came up to me, started climbing all over me, and sat on my lap. It was very playful. It was a new teaching venue for me. We just got right into it, and it was wonderful. I ended our chat with a gong meditation. I told the children to watch the sound of the gong, see where it went, and follow it there. I told them this might bring them closer to Buddha—to God.

The next week, I spoke with the mother of one of the children, and this is what her nine-year-old had told her about that experience. He said, "I watched the sound of the gong disappear, and I followed it. I went there, and you know what, Mom? When I went there, I didn't feel I was *closer* to God or Buddha—I *was* God." As it says in the Bible, "From the mouths of babes." This is something we all know, but we've forgotten. Sometimes, it is the teacher's job just to remind us what we've forgotten.

Speaking of teaching and teachers, you personally have been exposed to some of the masters of the time. You were taught by Dilgo Khyentse Rinpoche, who was probably the greatest living Dzogchen master when he was alive, as well as Kalu Rinpoche and Nyoshul Khenpo Rinpoche. What was it like to be taught by them?

I had the good fortune to land in the Himalayas and be there throughout most of the 1970s. I was very lucky to be with such teachers, and also with Dudjom Rinpoche and some female lamas—although they were few and far between. They were all very gracious and kind to me. I can never repay what they gave me. They returned to me my inner spiritual heritage.

Student–teacher relations is a big issue for us today. I don't want to give the impression that if you don't meet the great masters, you can't experience freedom, joy, unconditional love, and nirvanic peace. My teachers encouraged me to question, to find out for myself, to have confidence in myself. I felt when I met my gurus that they were like mirrors, reflecting back to me my highest true nature. That's what the dharma is about. Buddhism is the study of the self. To study self is to forget the self; this is the teaching of Dudjom Rinpoche.

A clear teacher, an enlightened mirror, accurately reflects our true nature—which we cannot usually appreciate through our own distorted self-concepts. We lose touch with who and what we really are, so the dharma is a mirror, the practice is a mirror, and the teacher is a mirror through which we can find ourselves. We value and treasure these mirrors, but we don't necessarily have to become mirror collectors. We find mirrors everywhere—our child's eyes are a mirror, a raindrop is a mirror, the unconditional love we share with our pets is a mirror—and they are all reflections of our Buddha nature. The Buddha energy is everywhere, manifesting through everything at every moment. The Buddha comes through the teacher to us so that it can awaken within us. That is the Buddha within.

So basically we all have access to this, and it is not necessary to be with a master to find the Buddha within?

Some of us are self-taught, and some of us are taught by others. It was a remarkable event when the dam burst in 1959, and the cloistered lake of timeless Tibetan wisdom came pouring down on us. We received, undiluted, all of this wisdom from impeccable embodiments of Buddhist tradition—the grand old lamas who were fully trained in Tibet. This has flowed down to us, and we are still drinking from that vast reservoir. But there are plenty of wise people in each of our lives, and we have inner wisdom that we can access. We can also go directly to Buddha—or to God or to our saints—through prayer and affirmation.

To find our true nature, I emphasize not only Buddha, but also dharma, which is the teaching, and sangha, which is the community, as crucial learning factors for us today. We have the Buddha.

The Buddha is everywhere. We have dharma. The dharma teachings and books are everywhere. But do we have a sangha in the West? Do we have a community, a spiritual kinship? I think that is something to develop and learn from and rely on these days, along with the teacher and the teaching. That is the threefold jewel—Buddha, dharma, and sangha. Teacher, teaching, and spiritual community. Buddha, in this case, refers not just to the person, but to the inner Buddha in which we find sanctuary. And dharma is the teaching, the truth. It's not just Buddhas and Buddhist teaching. It is the truth that speaks to us, the truth that we know is real for us. Sangha is living truly, in kinship and interconnection with the world, with the earth as well as the beings in it. That's community. It's not just the Buddhist community, the New Age community, or our friends, but true community. That is the refuge, the sanctuary, we find in Buddha, dharma, and sangha.

You mentioned the eightfold path earlier, and one of the aspects of the eightfold path is right livelihood, right work. Many of us are concerned about what we do for a living, and many of us are concerned about finding the right work—work that blends with personal passions and personal desires. Can you speak to that issue?

That's a very timely issue for all of us, and one I am working on myself. It is a kind of koan. How do we find our "right" work? How do we find work that we love, not just work we want to get away from at 5:00 P.M. on Friday so we can live our real life on the weekend? What is our impeccable vocation—not just right livelihood? What is our true vocation? We each need to find and live our true vocation. We need to find our passion and love what we're doing so that we don't just stop doing it at some arbitrary time. That's where the dharma lives.

It's a challenge to find our own true vocation, to find what really enlivens us—not just enlightens us—and connects us to others and our world. Even if we are alone, we're connected to others. Even if we are with others, we are alone. In other words, we must find the right balance between the inner and the outer life. And we must find a balance between the work we do for money and the work we do for love. We can discern these differences if we look honestly at our own lives. Of course, we can also do work to make money—that's part of the reason to work. It may not be the whole reason, but we don't have to pretend that money has nothing to do with it. It's not the money we need, but it's the shelter and the food that it brings for us and our families. So all this is part of impeccable vocation or right livelihood, which is a very important part of the eightfold path.

For those of us who have trouble finding three hours to devote to solitude, it is pretty impressive that you did two three-year, three-month, three-day retreats in the Tibetan tradition. What was your original motivation, and why did you go back and do it a second time?

We all say we don't have time, and I also hear myself saying it these days as I travel around and teach. And I am busy—we all are—but we can create time. We all have the same amount of time. It's how we choose to use it. I was fortunate that my search took me at a young age, and I was flexible. I didn't have that many commitments, so I could live like a monk in monasteries and stay in Asia for a long time and then do three-year retreats and so on. How long does it really take to awaken the spirit? Three years, three minutes, or one second of love or grace or blessing? It's different for everyone.

My principal teacher, Kalu Rinpoche, and Gyalwa Karmapa really emphasized that we do this three-year retreat. It was the way to get the full curriculum training for a lifetime of practice. So I was very inspired and prepared to do that. The first three-year retreat was really easy for me. It was wonderful. It was so rich, and the greatest teachers of Tibetan Buddhism, in my opinion, were teaching us. Khyentse Rinpoche, Dudjom Rinpoche, and Nyoshul Khenpo all lived there. Tulku Pema Wangyal and others visited. It was also very intense being a monk and living in a cell, sleeping sitting up, doing 100,000 mantras in a month, and any number of different practices. But I really loved devoting myself wholeheartedly to what I love, to doing what I was interested in.

I can still remember how I would go out for a meal, come back and sit down, and still be on the same page of my chant book. I would just pick it up again; there were no vacations or weekends or holidays. It was a cloistered three-year retreat in the forest in southern France, in the Dordogne valley, a beautiful place near the prehistoric cave sites of Cro-Magnon man. There were 22 people in that retreat. One of the most important things I learned from the experience was that you don't necessarily like everybody, but you can learn to love everybody. We all want and need more or less the same things, and that has helped me since then. After that, I had the opportunity to do it again. I loved the meditation practices, my teachers, and the teaching so much that I didn't feel there was anything else to do at that time, so I spent most of the '80s there. Altogether, I spent nine years in that retreat center.

You actually went to Tibet in 1990. What was that like?

Going to Tibet was a wonderful experience; it was also a sad experience. I had the opportunity to go with my teacher, Khyentse Rinpoche, Nyoshul Khenpo Rinpoche, and others. It was our sadhana to consecrate the oldest monastery in Tibet. Nyoshul Rinpoche was doing the pujas and so on. It was so sad how all the old Tibetans came. They hadn't seen any lamas for 30 years because of communist Chinese oppression. Rinpoche was up all night listening to their stories and asking about the old relatives, because he hadn't been there since 1959. It was inspiring, also. I hadn't really idealized Tibet, because I felt the best of Tibet was already in my life—that is, the teachers and the teachings and the practice at the monasteries. But Tibet is a very sacred land. It is the roof of the world, and it was a pure environment, ecologically speaking. The spirit of the people is indomitable, even after more than 30 years of communist oppression. They still have faith in dharma and so on. It was really remarkable, and it inspired me to see my own life more objectively and realize how easily I give up when the going gets rough.

What was it like for Nyoshul Khenpo going back after 30 years?

It was very moving for him, too. For the first time, he said, he didn't have a headache, and his psychic channels were straight and aligned, so it was healthy, and a good homecoming for him. He felt connected. He has been ill in the last decades, so it was a very healing experience—or maybe a reconciliation for him on some level. And we made a good pilgrimage to different places together. He has gone back again since then, and we're involved in building some hospitals for him in eastern Tibet, in the district called Kham, which has actually been annexed as part of China. Some of his relatives and people are still there and are relying on him as a lama and a leader to help them, so we are trying to build some hospitals and infirmaries there at places he's chosen. The Chinese are generally cooperative with these kinds of human health projects. He's also trying to rebuild and support the monasteries, nunneries, and retreat centers there. As are many of the lamas exiled in other countries, he is trying to keep alive the spirit of the people and the dharma in their own beleaguered country of Tibet, currently part of China.

For those of us who can't take a three-year retreat or visit Tibet, how do we become more conscious or more aware of who we are? And is it true that as we become more concerned about our own personal awareness, we somehow lose our social awareness or social concern?

Self-awareness training is available everywhere—through books, teachers, classes, meditation centers, and so on. But just stop where you are right now, put everything down, and have a total moment of pure presence. That can grow into a life of spiritual presence. As for losing our social awareness when we become self-aware, I don't think that has to happen. In fact, there is a whole new movement in Buddhism today called engaged Buddhism. Rather than practicing reclusive Buddhism in caves and mountaintops and deserts, this is Buddhism engaged with life, with human rights, with society. Leaders such as Thich Nhat Hanh, Sulak Sivaraksa, Mahatma Gandhi, Schweitzer, and others are big inspirations, and also there are traditional examples in the literature.

In some ways, that really seems to be our challenge, to bring our spiritual path into the world.

It's always good to get away and get more perspective on where we are, but we also have to invest energy and awareness in our community. I have been much inspired by some of the altruistic, loving activities of people who are not religious. They do not call it religion; they do it out of basic humanity, out of love, out of unselfishness, out of feeling connected with others. They work with abused children, victimized women, underprivileged people in Africa and the developing countries, and with the disenfranchised. This kind of work can make one more spiritual. This is the great compassion that is inseparable from wisdom that we often call love. The spiritual life doesn't have to take us away from anything. It can bring us back to oneness with everything, and help us become responsible guardians for the planet and all who inhabit it.

❖❖❖

EPILOGUE

Surya Das reminds us that Buddhism is much more than a religion. It's a new outlook on life. As a Westerner raised in Judaism, who immersed himself in both Hinduism and Buddhism in great depth, he is able to apply the Eastern concepts to a Western context in practical ways, and we are the beneficiaries. Enlightenment is no longer "out there" somewhere, but can become part of our everyday life. The essential goodness of who we are becomes paramount. Spiritual community, spiritual teachers, right work, creating time, meditation practice, and more are addressed in a clear and simple manner. In the end, all of life is spiritual, and our task is to see the connections and live that wisdom.

❖❖❖ ❖❖❖

CHAPTER NINE

It's All in Your Mind

Lama Tulku Thondup Rinpoche and Michael Toms

PROLOGUE

*W*estern science is now confirming that the mind and body are not separate—that thoughts and emotions influence physical health. To Tibetan Buddhists, this connection is ancient history and is an integral aspect of their philosophy. They have developed a technology of the mind that allows them to use the mind-body connection to heal both emotional and physical disease. Tulku Thondup Rinpoche exemplifies this approach to living.

Tulku Thondup has been a visiting scholar at Harvard University and lives in Cambridge, Massachusetts. He has written and published many books on Tibetan Buddhism, including Masters of Meditation and Miracles, Enlightened Journey, The Practice of Dzogchen, *and* The Healing Power of Mind: Simple Meditation Exercises for Health, Well-being, and Enlightenment.

❖❖❖

MICHAEL TOMS: You grew up and were raised in Tibet, and your parents were nomads, weren't they? Tell us what that was like for you.

TULKU THONDUP RINPOCHE: My parents were nomads, and I was born in a tent. We had to live on animals and dairy products. Since animals need grass to survive, we had to move four times a year to accommodate their needs. We were the only family living in a small valley, and in a way, that might seem like a very primitive life. But in another way, it was peaceful and joyful. It allowed one to discover what a meaningful life is. In those days, I didn't realize how valuable that was, but now, when I think back, I can really appreciate it. Of course, the modern world and modern technology brought us so much richness and so many benefits, and I appreciate all of them. But if I had been born in the West, I might not have discovered how rich that kind of life is, and I might not have realized the connection between body and mind.

When I was four or five years old, I was recognized as the rebirth of a great lama, and so my parents and grandfather sent me to the Dodrupchen Monastery. It was a famous monastery in eastern Tibet, belonging to the Nyingmapa school.

At the beginning of my fifth year, I was recognized as a Tulku, so I then took another year to grow up. At the beginning of my sixth year, I went to the monastery for good. After that, I saw my parents for a week once a year or every two years, but I never lived with my parents again. My teachers, the monks, were great scholars and great meditators, and they became my parents.

Growing up in a monastery, I didn't realize how valuable the experience was at the time. But the amazing thing was that from early morning till late at night, I would be studying or meditating.

Sometimes, of course, I would be playing, but most of the time was spent in study and meditation. The monks were wonderful, amazing people. They were much older than I was, but they understood what a child—a little boy—was like, so they were very kind and took care of me. It was a rich life, and I am grateful for what those monks did for me.

I had to leave the monastery at the age of 18, and I became a refugee living in India. As a refugee, my first concern was survival. It was very hard because I didn't speak English or Hindi or Nepali—the language of that area. It was a strange culture, and we weren't well prepared for the change in lifestyle. It was a struggle for two or three years, but then, slowly, because I had a good education and people were helpful, things got better. I got teaching jobs in a couple of Indian universities, and I taught for 13 years.

In 1980, I came to the United States. Harvard invited me as a visiting scholar, and so I taught at Harvard for a year. And then they asked me to stay for another year. I've been there since then.

What is your overall impression of the United States?

I think the most amazing thing about the United States is the individual freedom. I have been in other countries, and I've read about other countries, but there is no place where people have as much individual freedom as they have here. That is an amazing and wonderful treasure. Also, people are very nice. I have written in my book that wherever there is a problem or a disaster in the world, the Western people, and especially Americans, will be there to help. Of course, America is one of the richest countries in the world, which is a big plus, but there is also great love and compassion evident here, based on Judeo-Christian values.

BUDDHISM IN THE WEST

We also have a lot of emotional suffering in this country. We commonly use drugs to dull the pain. In some ways, these drugs cut us off from feelings of being depressed or discouraged or frustrated or angry—but the feelings don't go away. As prosperous as we are economically, we are even richer in emotional suffering. What about that?

I think that is the price of having more prosperity. If you are poor, you can't get drugs, but if you have money, you can. Of course, it is not a simple thing. It is a very big problem, and not just in the States. Drugs, alcohol, and these kinds of addictions are a problem everywhere. But in the West, especially in the States, these issues are brought quickly to everyone's attention through various media. Information about whatever is happening, whatever problems we are facing, gets out. Sometimes the media becomes too negative in its presentation, and this can be harmful, shutting down people's hopes and expectations. Maybe that is a price we have to pay, because the media can also help us become aware of problems. When an issue is presented in a way that really communicates with our hearts and minds, then we can take action. We can overcome any problem.

One of the things you discuss in The Healing Power of Mind *is learning to see problems as positive. What is the value of seeing problems in a positive way?*

We can realize many benefits by seeing our problems in a positive light. This is a Buddhist point of view, and although my book is based in Buddhist thought, one does not have to be a Buddhist to practice what I discuss. For example, if someone is rude to us or harsh with us, we can choose to see the situation as an opportunity to practice patience and tolerance. We need to recognize that the person who is being rude or harsh is probably driven by anger or jealousy. Those negative habits will ultimately have a detrimental effect on this person—or as a Buddhist would see it, that person is creating bad karma for his future. But when we choose to show compassion and practice tolerance and patience, this person's rudeness creates good karma for us. We can be grateful for this opportunity to strengthen ourselves and our lives through our positive actions. Any time we face problems, we need to look for a way to turn them to our advantage so that we may become stronger.

This relates directly to the experiences of some of the older Tibetan monks who spent many years in prison. In their remarks about how they survived prison, they indicated that they survived because they were able to see the positive aspects of their captivity. They didn't dwell on the negative side, and they didn't blame their jailers or their captors. Isn't that what you're describing?

Those lamas, as well as many ordinary people I've known, have had very difficult lives, but instead of blaming someone else, they say, "Oh, because of my own karma it happened to me, and because of the other person's bad karma, they had to do it. But I can't blame them." I'm not saying everyone thought that way, but many people chose to see their situations in that light. And they benefited from those positive thoughts. The amount we blame others is proportionate to the amount of hatred we create in ourselves. Negative emotions create more stress, more pressure, and the negative feelings perpetuate themselves. But if we can alter our perception of a situation so that we see even bad things in a positive way, we can create compassion, peace, and joy in our hearts and minds. Then, even though the situation is bad, we will be strengthened by it.

I use many different examples of this in my book. For instance, I talk about a lama who was practicing a particular

Buddhist meditation on great bliss, when he hit his head against a rock and began bleeding. Instead of feeling pain, however, he felt only bliss. We don't all have this kind of discipline, but we can strive for it.

You told another story in The Healing Power of Mind *about when you were in northern India with a group of friends. This was at the time when you were a refugee, and you didn't have many resources. You wanted to cook a meal, so you had gone off to look for firewood and some stones with which to build a fire, and you encountered an older monk in a little hovel. Can you tell us that story?*

When I talk about this monk, I still feel a tingling sensation throughout my body. I came across him while I was looking for firewood. He was cooking a meal, and he broke into a big smile when he saw me—like an old friend meeting me for the first time after many years. But I had never met him; we were strangers. He asked me what I was looking for, and I told him I was looking for fuels to make a tea, that I had just arrived here. So he said, "Oh, just sit here. There's not much, but we will share this meal." I saw that he was cooking a very small meal. I said, "No, I have some friends waiting over there. I have to go." Then he said, "Oh, then, when I finish cooking my meal, you take my stove." He was offering me the charcoal stove he was using. The amazing thing was that he was so poor and so old. There was hardly enough for him, but he wanted to share. Even though he didn't know me, he offered me his stove, which was almost his whole livelihood. But he trusted me. His big smile, the joy in his face, and the love in his voice—all these things made a big impact on me. I remember him very vividly.

Somehow, even in dire poverty, he was able to experience joy and happiness. Do you think that he was perfectly satisfied because of his positive outlook?

There was peace and joy and contentment in his mind, so day by day he was surviving. He was enjoying his life. That's why we generally dream about the future—we don't have a present. We don't live in the present moment. We can't enjoy our lives because we can only dream—or worry—about the future. But he was living in the present, enjoying it, and not worrying about what the future might hold. Of course, he had to prepare for the future to some extent, but his main focus was enjoying the present because he was content in his mind.

We have so much in the United States; we are so rich in material things. But even though we have all these material goods, products, services, and technologies, we are still unhappy. Can you speak to that condition?

I think that is one of the major problems we face here. Every day there are more goods and services available to us. We begin to think we can't survive without them. We constantly struggle to satisfy our material needs so that we don't have time to think about our spiritual needs. We forget to experience ourselves, our bodies, and we fail to discover how to bring peace and joy into our minds. We don't have time, and that is very damaging to the individual and to our society.

To eliminate the unhappiness or depression that comes from the stress of daily existence, we must make time to look within and try to understand the connection between mind and body. Healing or wellness could be different things for different people because of their different needs, but the most important aspect of it is to have peace, joy, and strength in our lives. And peace, joy, and strength are concepts created by the mind and feelings experienced by the mind. Therefore, we must use the mind to create and to experience them. With a peaceful, joyful, and strong mind, we can heal the problems of our physical body and day-to-day lives.

Mindfulness involves trying to be aware of every moment. Too often, we say something and then think, *Oh, what did I just say? Too bad I said that.* That illustrates a lack of mindfulness. Whatever we are going to say, we need to think about it first and then say it. Whatever we are going to do, we need to think about it first and then do it. Even when we are walking, we must be mindful of every step of life. Then, we will be fully aware and alive. Otherwise, our mind is one place while our body is doing something else.

We need to devote a little time each day to achieving mindfulness. Whether it's 5, 10, or 15 minutes a day, we need to allow ourselves that time. Once a day—first thing in the morning if possible—we need to take a few minutes just to sit quietly and think about something spiritual. We can meditate, watch our breathing, try to sense the feelings of the body, or use visualization techniques. Whatever technique we use, the intention is to bring our focus inward, to become aware of ourselves and our lives.

In my book, I describe many exercises, and most of them are based on four tools, the means of healing. Image is the first tool, and by that I mean a mental image or a visualization. When confronted with the task of visualization, many people tell me, "Oh, I can't visualize." But in a way, we all visualize to some extent. Every time we think, we couple that thought with a mental image. When we think of home, we see the image of our home; or when we think about a friend, we see the image of that friend in our mind. That's all visualization is. In this case, we create a visualization that is positive, one that is a source of peace, joy, and strength.

The second tool involves naming or thinking. After we create an image in our mind, we must think of it as positive and wonderful. If we don't think of this image as positive, as a source of joy, then it won't be helpful. So we have to think about the image in a certain way; we have to give it a positive name or designation in order to realize its power.

The third tool is feeling. We are all (especially in the West) very cerebral, and we are very good at thinking. By viewing concepts abstractly, intellectually, we cut ourselves off from feeling. Sometimes we just have to allow ourselves to respond viscerally to an idea. Especially if it is an idea we need to feel positive about. When we visualize a wonderful image and we *think* it is a wonderful source of healing, then we must also *feel* that it is a wonderful source of healing. If you don't feel it, then it's only a concept, and it won't make the same impact.

The fourth tool involves faith. We may have a wonderful image, a wonderful name for it, and a wonderful feeling about it, but we also have to believe that this image has the power to heal. If we doubt the healing ability of our image, then it will not work. Of course, believing is hard, but we have to try. We have to invest ourselves and our faith in the power of the image. If we do that, and try it again and again, then slowly the habit of believing will come to us. If we use these four tools, if we practice with them daily, then whatever positive healing exercises we do will be effective.

In the West, particularly in America, we are trained to doubt, trained to be skeptical. We are trained to be cynical. It's insidious, and it permeates our lives. Do you have any insights as to how we can cultivate the ability to really believe, to have faith, to trust?

The Buddha said, "Don't trust me; first, see for yourself—test for yourself. When you find something believable, then believe."

I think that is the point. I'm not suggesting that we should have blind faith. That's not what we are looking for. First, we have to examine these ideas, determine whether this is a worthy approach, or whether this is a proper way of meditating, of living, and so on. But when we decide that this is a worthwhile thing, then we have to trust; otherwise, we will never really be able to move forward.

It's important that we critically examine new concepts. We have to study an idea, learn about it, be critical of it, and reach our own conclusions about it. If we do that, and reach the conclusion on our own that an idea is valuable, then the trust will come. In meditations, many people reach a certain stage of experience where there's no need for words or approval. They just feel deep within themselves that "Yes, this is what I was looking for. Yes, this is truth."

It's interesting that you've spent a third of your life in Tibet, a third of your life in India, and now a third of your life in the United States. How would you compare your life in the United States with life in India and Tibet?

I think every phase of my life has been a spiritual learning experience. In Tibet, I grew up in a tradition that taught me the value of my mind, body, and everyday life in terms of peace, joy, and strength. And then in India, at first, I had a hard time surviving as a refugee, but I was able to get beyond that. I was able to study, learn different languages, and try to open my eyes outside of Tibet. In Tibet, I never heard a single word of English or anything. Only in the latter part of my life did I hear the name *America*. Living in India opened my eyes to the whole outside world. And then I came to the States, to the richness and the kindness of people here. In the States, I was able to produce some results out of what I went through. Now, I have published a few books, and these are something I can leave behind, some small repayment for all that my great teachers invested in me. Everyone has to leave, and when we leave, we want to leave something behind for friends and others. If I had stayed in India, I may not have published or produced these books. Writing, editing, and publishing them would have been more difficult. So for me, each phase of my life has allowed some new aspect of myself to reach fruition.

There's a section in your book where you focus on daily living activities, such as healing. You talk about work as a healing activity, but that's a difficult concept to grasp. Not all of us feel that work is a place where we can actually heal ourselves. Can you talk about that?

In order to find work a healing activity, we must first create peace, joy, and strength in our minds. Buddhists believe that we are all basically peaceful and joyful in our nature. We are like the ocean. At the bottom, the ocean is peaceful, calm, and clear. But on the top, there is turmoil—rolling waves and pollution. In the same way, the foundation of our mind is peaceful, calm, and clear. We all have that wonderful foundation. Maybe our lives are in turmoil on the surface—on the emotional or conceptual level. But by nature, we are all peaceful and joyful. If we can reach back to that foundation through meditation, through reflections, through feeling, through believing, as we discussed previously, then whatever work we do will become an expression of that peaceful foundation and energy. If we are not at peace in our minds, in our hearts, we will not find peace in our work.

Doing a five-minute meditation each morning can help bring about that sense of peace and joy. Then when we go to work, we can remind ourselves of our meditation and bring back that peaceful feeling from time to time—even if it's just for a couple of seconds. Gradually—maybe not today or tomorrow, but eventually—there will come a time when we can always feel our peaceful foundation, even when our work is in turmoil.

Sometimes we have so much work to do that we feel stressed and unhappy. We feel overwhelmed, saying, "Oh, I have too much work." But if we can turn that into a more positive way of thinking, if we can say, "Oh, how wonderful to have the opportunity to work," then the experience will become more rewarding. If we think of work as wonderful, label it as wonderful, and feel it as wonderful, then it will be transformed into an energy of joy, instead of becoming something burdensome.

What if you feel that you are being put under undue pressure or that you are being exploited in some way by your employer? What about that?

If this is the case, we need to keep two things in mind. First, if an employer is not treating us well, we have to deal with that person by talking to him or her. However, we can't allow ourselves to get upset. We can't deal with this problem on an emotional level. For instance, when we feel very angry with our employer, we need to realize that this is not a good time to discuss the issue. In the shanty they always say, "When you get angry, don't say anything, don't do anything, but remain as a piece of wood."

The next thing we have to do is learn to release our anger. We need to breathe deeply, feel the anger being expelled with each outgoing breath. Through visualization, through naming, through feeling, and through believing, we can release our anger. When we are calm, when the anger is gone, then we can think about how to deal with the situation practically. Any time we are angry or under emotional pressure, we can use these techniques to calm down. We can create peace in our hearts and minds and imbue everything we do with peace and joy and contentment.

❖❖❖

EPILOGUE

Again, the emphasis on mindfulness as the means to eliminate unhappiness, depression, or daily stress, appears. Tulku Thondup also provides the four tools of healing to assist us in our self-healing practice. The focus continues to be on our innate capacity to manifest positive change from within. The Buddha resides in each of us, and we have only to dispel the clouds preventing us from seeing our true nature. Changing our perspective and attitude about the pressures and challenges we encounter in everyday life into a more positive outlook will alter our experience of these things. Life will become more satisfying, and we will be more at peace.

❖❖❖ ❖❖❖

CHAPTER TEN

Tibetan Wisdom for the West

Robert Thurman
and Michael Toms

PROLOGUE

In 1959, the Dalai Lama was forced to leave Tibet because of the Chinese invasion. Since then, more than 100,000 refugees have joined him in exile. In Tibet itself, 1.3 million Tibetans have lost their lives, and more than 6,000 monasteries have been destroyed under Chinese rule. Despite the ongoing Chinese policy of eradicating the Tibetan culture inside Tibet, the Tibetan refugee community has flourished, in contrast to other refugee communities. The Dalai Lama has received the Nobel Peace Prize and has met, and is respected by, most of the world's major religious and secular leaders. Tibetan spiritual teachers have attracted large followings in many parts of the world. Numerous books detailing many aspects of Tibetan Buddhism have been published, including some bestsellers. In the following discussion, Robert Thurman explores the relevance of Tibetan Buddhism in the modern world.

Thurman is the chair of the Department of Religion at Columbia University, where he is Jey Tsong, Khapa, professor of Indo-Tibetan Buddhist studies. Well known as an interpreter of Buddhist ideas for a Western audience, he is the president of the Tibet House in New York, the cultural and educational institution that he co-founded with actor Richard Gere. Thurman is the author of several books on Tibet, including Wisdom and Compassion, The Sacred Art of Tibet, The Central Philosophy of Tibet, *and* Essential Tibetan Buddhism.

❖❖❖

MICHAEL TOMS: *Why do you think that Tibetan Buddhism has become so popular in the Western world?*

ROBERT THURMAN: First of all, I'm not sure it's quite that popular. I think that Christianity is alive and well in its various forms. Islam is spreading more powerfully in America than Buddhism, and worldwide, Islam is a much more vibrantly growing religion than Buddhism. It might be more accurate to say that some of the main ideas and themes of Tibetan Buddhism appeal to many people who would not officially call themselves Tibetan Buddhists. In that sense, it has become very popular. One of the attractions is the Buddhist belief in using the power of the mind to change our lives. The Buddhist tradition actually provides practical methods and exercises that we can use every day to change how we perceive reality. That seems to be important to many people.

There seem to be a lot of misconceptions about Buddha and Buddhism, but particularly about the Buddha. Non-Buddhists ask, "Is this God? Is this comparable to Jesus? Just who is the Buddha?" How do you respond to that?

It has been said that whoever thinks he sees the Buddha does not see the Buddha. In other words, we should be guarded in thinking that we can say exactly who the Buddha is. There are many different visions of the Buddha. I feel that the Buddha was a being who was constantly changing. When people met him during the 45 years of his teaching, he would appear slightly different to each person. Of course, people perceive each other very differently, and you get different descriptions of the same person. But I think a being such as the Buddha could actually alter himself to fit the needs of others.

The Buddha supposedly became perfectly aware of the nature of reality and perfectly aware of the nature of self. He was therefore able to remove the limitations of personal manifestation so that he could actually manifest whatever was most helpful to those around him. Naturally, he would be perceived in a multifaceted way. The impact of that ability was so great that for about 200 or 300 years he would be represented in art as a wheel, a footprint, or a tree. There was no anthropomorphic representation of him. But after a few hundred years, he was shown in human form.

The most important name for the Buddha in the Buddhist tradition is Shasta—as in Mount Shasta. *Shasta* means "teacher" in Sanskrit. Buddhists believe that the most miraculous thing about the Buddha was his ability to teach people to understand their lives, to learn why they suffer, and then to remove the causes of that suffering to find real happiness.

In Essential Tibetan Buddhism, *you wrote that the Buddha had achieved a state of omniscience, and this state would be comparable to knowing all things everywhere, eternally. The difference between that and the Christian God is that the Buddha denied any powers of creation and omnipotence. Can you expand on that?*

The Buddha said that he was not omnipotent and not in control of everything. He may have been omniscient, but I think we have to be careful about how we define the concept of omniscience. For example, if we ask someone, "Are you a vegetarian?" and the person says, "I'm omnivorous," that doesn't mean he is, at that precise moment, eating everything in the universe. It means that the person is potentially ready to eat *anything*. Similarly, omniscience means that if a Buddha being—an enlightened, awakened being—wanted to know something, and put his mind to it, he would be able to understand it thoroughly and immediately. However, it doesn't mean that the knowledge is being entertained all the time, every second. This is a key point.

The Buddha, unlike most religious founders, did not set out to discover the nature of reality. Nor did he set out to discover some other being who knew what that nature was. What Buddha discovered was that he could know—and that any other human being could know—everything he needed to know about how to be truly happy and capable of making others happy. All he had to do was open his heart and his basic energy. He discovered that the purpose of life is to educate yourself, to know your state of being thoroughly, and then you can really be well. That was his major contribution. This differs from the Christian concept of God in that Buddha believed we each have to do things for ourselves rather than thinking that if we just believe in some greater being, that being will do things for us.

Would you say that Buddhism doesn't believe in the concept of God, but it believes in the nature of God?

I think that is a fair statement. We have to be careful. When we talk about the concept of God, of course we mean the idea of God as the monotheistic creator. It's important for people (especially people in a theistic society) to know this nowadays so that they don't feel too nervous about Buddhism. The 19th-century European scholars who translated Buddhist tenets into European languages wrongly characterized Buddhism as atheistic. Westerners were upset by this and thought of Buddhists as just materialists or something. But this is not true. Buddhism is theistic in the sense that Buddha believed in the existence of gods—many of them.

In a traditional account, Buddha met one of the Indian gods, Brahma, who was believed at the time to be the creator. Just as Moses met God in the form of a burning bush or a whirlwind, the Buddha met Brahma. The difference was that Brahma said, "Hey, I didn't do it. I'm not guilty. I didn't make it all like this. Please tell the people that I'm not responsible for their state." Brahma was anxious for the Buddha to begin his teaching and said, "Well, I don't mind if some people think I'm in control of everything if it makes them feel secure. The problem is that if they have a lot of misfortune, they naturally want to blame me. But it's not my fault. It's their karma; it's their own fate, their own destiny, their own previous actions in previous lives that causes the suffering. I am a powerful force of energy and love and joy in the universe. My energy does keep atoms dancing, but I didn't originally start the universe, and I don't have full control over it by any means—even over myself. I could lose my power at some time in the future. So Buddha, if you understand how any being—including a god—can find a way to true happiness, by all means, teach it to the world."

Buddha can't be said to be atheistic, since he and the Buddhists think that he actually talked with the gods. In India they call him the "teacher of humans and gods." Buddha is the force of intelligence in the universe. Some people think Buddha was a pessimist because he talked about suffering. But he also talked about being able to go beyond suffering to achieve happiness by discovering the nature of reality. He gave us the means to achieve happiness by our own efforts, by our own understanding.

The unique thing about the Tibetan culture—before the Chinese takeover—was that the people actually believed there were living Buddhas among them, and that it was possible for them as individuals to attain to the same level. What are your thoughts on that?

That was the first thing told to me when I encountered Tibetan Buddhism. Historically, most other cultures in the Buddhist tradition, although they deeply venerated the Buddha and became very devout in their practice, felt that one had to have lived in ancient India and met the Buddha before one could become a Buddha. Either that or one had to have been in a special kind of karma, and people now—living in the dark ages—can't achieve it. But the Tibetans never got into that dark-age consciousness because they had living Buddhas with them. Personally, I think that the tradition was totally alive in India until the end of the first millennium when the foreign invasions began. India was such a rich and open country, and it was vulnerable, so these living Buddhas took the heart of Buddhism and hid it in Tibet. Perhaps it is a little fatalistic of me, or a little wishful thinking on my part, but I like to think they were keeping it for the world today. I like to think that they were keeping it for a time when the world most desperately needs the living heart of intelligence and goodness.

You wrote an extraordinary explanation about the tragedy of Tibet in which Vajrapani incarnated as Mao Tse-tung. Would you relate that extraordinary story and explain what has happened in recent years in Tibet?

The Tibetan vision of reality, as I've come to understand it, is, in a way, the most super-positive vision of human evolution that one could imagine. It connects to the Shambala or Shangri-la idea. That is not to say, of course, that Tibet itself was Shangri-la. Tibetans are fully aware it was not. It had many flaws and faults. It was still a developing society. There were many injustices, problems, and much suffering. Tibet is a harsh environment at its high altitude.

On a surface level, our planet's history seems horrible—filled with wars, death, destruction, and plagues. But if we consider the underlying level of the world as a kind of culture in which beings can mature toward enlightenment—and that doesn't mean living just one life, but experiencing many lives, deaths, and rebirths—in that view, the world becomes the optimal possible evolutionary environment. It's like a greenhouse for souls that are seeking liberation. That is Tibet's vision, because Tibetans have come to have such respect for the power of the enlightened being. They feel that because of Buddha's compassion and his far-reaching methodology of helping humans evolve, on an underlying level, the planet is actually going in a positive direction.

Within that framework, then, we can take a rather different view of the ongoing Tibetan holocaust. Since 1949, which marked the first invasion of Tibet by the Chinese People's Liberation Army, the Chinese goal has been to assimilate the Tibetan people. This is known in human-rights parlance as genocide by assimilation, or genocide by population transfer. The Tibetans, however, have chosen to see this as an experience from which they can benefit. They believe that history had reached a stage where people were getting confused and were about to destroy all dharma institutions—the gateways through which people find intellectual and spiritual liberation from suffering. Therefore, out of compassion, the Bodhisattvas emanated a very powerful Bodhisattva in the form of fierce-looking blue Vajrapani, who held a thunderbolt scepter in his hand and came preemptively to destroy the Buddhist institutions so that in their confusion the people could not lash out and get all the bad karma. The vajapani destroyed things in such a way that it brought people around to the heart of the dharma. Out of that came a renewed energy toward the dharma. It has been suggested that the vajapani was reborn as Mao Tse Tung, and the destruction and miserable living conditions that were a result of the Chinese invasions served to throw people back to the original resources of their hearts and minds.

People go on and on about the great Chinese economic boom, but actually the Chinese are in this state of rushing after money blindly because their family lives were shattered for several generations by all the social upheaval. The Chinese people have lost basic trust, and they've lost a basic tenderness and affection. They were so emotionally traumatized and brutalized that they think there is nothing left but chasing after money or a Mercedes or something. The Dalai Lama always says that his heart totally goes out to the Chinese people, and he hopes the Chinese people can recover their own great spiritual traditions—their own dharma.

Of course, we in the West have also fallen prey to this materialism because of our own terrible karma. Look at the genocide we practiced on the Native Americans, and we enslaved the African Americans, and we're still putting them in ghettos and in prisons. We still condone violence within our families, allowing brutality and abuse of children and spouses. We come from a long lineage of violent conquerors, but those of us who are trying to transform have realized the futility of that.

The Buddhists and the Dalai Lama are quick to say that this doesn't mean we can just sign up with a new religious movement and think that now everything will be fine. If we are selfish and having a miserable time, we aren't going to recover just by saying

Tibetan Wisdom for the West

we're Buddhists. So they don't want to convert us. They don't want to start a religious competition or a religious conflict. What they want us to do is employ whatever method we can to cure ourselves, to bring our negative side under restraint, to heighten and intensify our positive side, and most of all to develop the scope and power of our understanding. The more we can do that, the better off everyone will be.

I think somehow that's happening in America, but I don't like to call it Buddhism. I don't like to say that Buddhism is taking over America. I think that is really dangerous. We want Christians to do this with their own hearts and minds, based on their own resources. If they can reinforce Christian love with a little Buddhist method, so be it. God doesn't mind, and Jesus wouldn't mind a little Buddhist methodology mixed in.

It would certainly be better than what we currently have in the West, which is a sort of antireligious, psychological way of thinking. This school of thought says that we shouldn't put too much strain on ourselves; it is too hard on the ego. We shouldn't control our anger; we shouldn't do this or that because it will be bad for our mental/emotional health. But I think these psychologies often tend to work against our spiritual side. Buddhism, on the other hand, can help by providing psychological bridges that will reinforce the spiritual side. We want to see this happen within Christianity, within Buddhism, and within Islam, if possible, and not as a competitive movement.

An example of that might be seen in the relationship between the Dalai Lama and Thomas Merton and how they met at the level of experience, not at the level of dogma. Could you speak to that?

We were with His Holiness last summer at Gethsemani, Thomas Merton's monastery in Kentucky. It was the first time His Holiness had visited there. He spoke movingly of how Merton opened his eyes to his Buddhist chauvinism about Christianity. He said that when he met Merton, he realized here was a man who was not a Buddhist, but just from his own resources and his own tradition had really become a holy man, a wise man. It was revelatory to the Dalai Lama, and it was tremendously encouraging.

When we are locked into a world view such as fundamentalist Buddhism, fundamentalist Christianity, or fundamentalism of any kind, we become intolerant, thinking that if others aren't doing exactly what we're doing, then they are lost. How impoverished is that view! Whereas if we suddenly discover that others are able to get to where we think we'd like to be on their own resources, then that reinforces us. As one Christian minister I know said, "God is wiser than any of his religions." We could say of Buddhism, "Buddha's methods are more miraculous and more far reaching than just what is within the Buddhist religion." We need to have more faith in each other and realize that we all are striving for the same things.

The visit to Gethsemani occurred in the summer of 1996. Tell us about that since you were there. How was it?

It was a wonderful experience. His Holiness was moved, thinking back on his youthful meetings with Thomas Merton in the '60s and also feeling the sad tragedy of Merton's premature death, but what had begun then, continues today. Christian and Buddhist monks were interacting in a lovely way. Trappist monks and nuns from other monasteries and nunneries realized that they could feel the holiness, the love, the respect, and the sort of possibility of reinforcement from the Buddhist tradition, yet they didn't have to feel they were opposed to each other or competing in any way. Everyone had the same basic sensibility about love being all powerful in the world, and they realized the value of devoting their lives to love.

I also enjoyed giving talks in Louisville to sort of inform people about Tibet and the Dalai Lama. People would come up after the talk and tell me, "Well, you know, I lived in such-and-such a town near the monastery, and Tom Merton used to come by when he was delivering vegetables for the monks. He would have a glass of beer with us. He would chat, and he was a jolly man—don't think he was all misery and hair shirts. He was one of the most cheerful people." They would tell me these lovely anecdotes of their encounters with Merton, what a fine person he was, and how much they loved him. I was amazed at how beloved he still is in that area.

As a Tibetan Buddhist scholar, and someone reputed to be the first American Tibetan Buddhist monk, and having had the Dalai Lama as your teacher, from your perspective just who is the Dalai Lama?

He is believed to be and has the signs of being the reincarnation of Avalokitesvara, which is the sort of apotheosis of great compassion—universal compassion for all beings. Iconographically, Avalokitesvara is depicted as a Bodhisattva with 1,000 arms and 11 heads, with eyes in the palms of his hands. The 1,000 arms symbolize extending a helping hand to all beings, and the eyes symbolize doing so intelligently and carefully. The Dalai Lama is believed to be the incarnation of this.

After 1,000 years of cultivating themselves with the Buddhist educational method, it is amazing that Tibetans would reach a point where they would have the vision to demilitarize their country and stop their warfaring tendencies—which they very definitely had. They were tremendous conquerors and very militaristic before Buddhism. It took them 1,000 years to stop being militaristic, but between 600 and 1700, they learned that lesson. They demilitarized, and they embraced the idea that human life offered an opportunity for enlightenment.

Tibetans came to the conclusion that if they put their whole effort into seeking enlightenment and didn't waste time fighting other people, aggrandizing themselves, or producing things that just piled up unnecessary wealth, that a lot of progress could be made in life, and one could really achieve a higher quality of being. They got so deeply into that vision that they organized their society around the idea of maximizing the amount of time spent seeking enlightenment. One element of that involved turning over their government to their messiah figure, who was to be reincarnated again and again. So instead of electing a president who might or might not be honest, who might or might not have special interests, they chose to give that post to their highest religious figure.

The Tibetans wanted to embed religious virtues and spiritual development into daily life. That's how, in the last three centuries, the Dalai Lama got to be the ruler of Tibet. He was invited as the head monk to be the ruler, and then succeeded himself by being reincarnated. It's an amazing social institution. All Buddhist societies believe totally in reincarnation—that beings are reborn whether willingly or not, consciously or not. But the idea that a person would do so consciously, and that a person would devote himself to continuously running a country in an honest, selfless way, is a unique Tibetan innovation. So the Dalai Lama is not only a religious leader of Tibet, but a secular leader as well.

The present Dalai Lama is the only one I've known personally. I think because he was there when Tibetan society was shattered by the Chinese invasion and he saw the communist attempt to assimilate the people and destroy the religion, he put a different level of effort into realizing the meaning of suffering, impermanence, wisdom, and compassion. He suffered the loss of his country, he suffered the loss of many people who were dear to him, and he suffered the loss of many things of beauty that he was responsible for in his culture, such as 6,250 monasteries. He therefore put an extra level of effort into practicing his own teaching, and I think he has become an immensely wise and compassionate person. I've really seen the difference.

When I first met him in the early '60s, I would go to him and say, "Give me some teachings. I want enlightenment." He would say, "Let's talk about nuclear physics," or "Let's talk about Freud," or "Let's talk about the American democratic system." I was the second person he knew who was fluent in Tibetan and with whom he could discuss the West. Heinrich Harrer was the other person with whom he could speak Tibetan. A film based on Heinrich Harrer's book, *Seven Years in Tibet*, was released in the fall of 1997. The Dalai Lama knew a bit of English then, but it was much better to hear these things interpreted in his native tongue—although it was not easy to explain Freud in Tibetan. For me the physics and the technical things were even harder to explain because I was grounded in humanities. So I saw him then as a fellow student, a little bit my senior, and although I could see people loving him and believing in him, it was hard for me to really understand his charisma because of my closeness to him. He did ordain me, but he wanted me to be instructed by the older teachers.

I saw him again in the '70s for a long period of time, and then in the '80s. Each time there was incremental growth in his actual manifestations. I mean, maybe he was Buddha from previous lives—I don't know. When I saw him in the '70s, I thought of him as a master philosopher, a deep thinker on the nature of emptiness and all the technicalities of Buddhist metaphysics and epistemology, which are very complicated and very difficult. In the '80s, he did a lot of Tantric retreats, but he was blocked by

Kissinger from visiting the United States for about seven years—the government wouldn't give him a visa. The Chinese tried to block his entry into European countries by threatening a country's government if the Dalai Lama was given permission to visit—so he was also blocked from going around the world. He therefore turned that energy into staying at home and offering tremendous retreats. I began to feel his Tantric charisma energy in the '80s, and from then on.

He has used the tools of his tradition fully, and he has become the best living proof of the value and power of Buddhism. One can feel that he is a Buddha-like being, and he is dignified and inspirational, but he isn't pompous. He tells us, "I'm a simple monk," and that's really who he is. So he has this flexibility of personality and is not rigidly stuck on being a higher authority to whom we are to pay homage. That is what enlightenment is supposed to be—the realization of "identitylessness." He definitely has that ability. When he visits the White House, for example, and when he leaves, he is just as friendly with the chauffeur, the bodyguard, the dog, or the cat as he is with the president and the First Lady and the child. He pays total attention to everybody at every level, and I have to admire that tremendously.

This was a teaching that previously was only given very rarely in Tibet itself. It exemplifies the dispersal of some of these esoteric teachings that took 20 years as a monk in Tibet to even get the chance to hear. Now, one can go to a weekend seminar with a Tibetan lama and receive these teachings. What about that?

Although we can get an introduction to these teachings in a weekend seminar, we have to dedicate speech and mind to these teachings over a period of time to realize them fully and to embody them in our lives. We have to realize that to transform ourselves still requires a lifelong commitment to a certain way of living. On the other hand, the essence of Tibetan Buddhism is the idea that if we do put our total energy into it, if we make it a priority, we can really rise above things and transform ourselves. I think one of the reasons that some Tibetan teachers like to teach in the West is because we are not bound by the standard Buddhist conventions. We have our pragmatic American attitude; we are ready to get somewhere and try something, thinking that we can get results. They see that, and they like that.

We have lost many things in this culture, and we've inherited the negative actions of past generations, such as the slaughter of Native Americans and the enslavement of African Americans. Because of that, we are driven in a special way to want transformation; therefore, when we hear the dharma and find tools to do it, we will generate a tremendous worldwide renaissance. That doesn't mean we're all going to become sort of card-carrying Buddhists, but we are going to become more feeling, thinking, and understanding of human beings no matter what our denominational connections are. We are going to change this world finally, and we are going to make it something really great. That is the Tibetan prophecy, and the Tibetan view of Shangri-la, and I hope it happens.

As I grow older, I get a little discouraged to see what the state machinery is up to around the world. I see the collusion of our own government with the current dictators of China who are suppressing their people, and I see the collusion of the United Nations in this behavior. Even though everyone says they want peace, the Dalai Lama is not being invited to the U.N. Here's a man whose people have been violently wronged. He has lost his country, his people are still undergoing oppression, and yet he teaches that we should be liberated from this, and we should appeal to our hearts.

The Dalai Lama is not asking for military support, he is simply asking for our moral support, for our honesty, for our taking a stand against all this corruption. That is all he is asking. But we are so indoctrinated to the militaristic way and the way of violence that instead of responding to his request, we say, "Well, they must not be serious about wanting freedom." Or maybe we tell ourselves that nothing really bad is happening to the Tibetan people, because they are not willing to kill themselves and a lot of other people for their cause. So instead of giving our moral support, we gave missiles to the Afghanistan people, who, once they got rid of the Russians, began killing each other—which is what the Dalai Lama doesn't want the Tibetans to do.

We should reward this leader who is trying to make peace the method for attaining what he wants—not just paying lip service to it as a means of justifying violence. Instead of ignoring him, as the world leaders are presently doing, we should rise up in one voice and say to them, "You cannot ignore this man; this man is necessary for our future as well as the Chinese and the Tibetan people's future."

We certainly don't read about this in the newspaper or see it on the television news.

With all the Jiang Zemin hype and the death of Deng Xiaoping hype, no one mentions that Deng led the invasion of Tibet, and Deng had a personal obsession with keeping Tibet and not ever letting up an inch and never talking to the Dalai Lama. Jiang Zemin, for whom we're planning a 21-gun salute, is going to come around with the pandas and meet with Clinton. This is a man who is presiding over a policy that keeps Tibet under Chinese rule. He is actively pursuing this genocide on the Tibetans. This is a human rights violation; the Chinese have no more right there than Hussein had in Kuwait, and yet we are inviting him to our White House. This is something that the press choose never to mention. People talk about constructive engagement; the press never mentions that this is what people used to say when they were coddling the apartheid regime. When we stopped giving business to the oppressors in South Africa, then they stopped their repression, and Nelson Mandela is there as a result. It's unconscionable that we are not doing the same thing about the oppressors of Tibet.

When I was younger and first started as a monk, I enjoyed Tibetan Buddhism—the reasoning, the philosophy, the meditation, and the rituals. But as far as the situation in Tibet was concerned, I put it out of my mind, thinking it was a lost cause and we couldn't help. I was being dualistic there, and it took me 15 years to realize that if we see a certain principle in a thing, even if it looks difficult or impossible, we are bound to speak up for it.

What do you think of a book called The Coming Conflict with China*?*

The book is by Richard Bernstein Ross Monroe, and it is a very useful reevaluation of the American sellout—not to China, because China's full of 1.3 billion people whom we love—but to the 25 men of the Chinese Politburo who basically are gangsters. They are like the Chinese mafia, and they do still control all their people's lives, and they suppress their people's aspirations. This book really shows not only how unconscionable, but how dangerous, the Politburo is for our future. It is a wonderful book.

Here in the United States we pride ourselves on our individualism—individual rights, being an individual, all of that. In the Tibetan tradition, there is this master–disciple relationship. We also have demonized cults and the whole idea of giving ourselves over to someone else. How do you feel about the master–student relationship.

This is a complex issue, of course, but let me start by saying that Buddhism is actually the most individualistic tradition that there is—much more so even than American individualism. Buddhism teaches that each individual comes from a past history of evolutionary action that is called karma, so that each individual earns his or her own human life. Our parents were kind enough to allow us to reincarnate with their genes, but basically we earned the ability to be attracted to the human form. On an evolutionary basis, we worked our way up to that level; therefore, it is something we've earned. So for someone in a collective to tell us that we must use that embodiment, that intelligence, to produce things in a factory, to work on a farm, to fight in an army, or to believe in a cult is contrary to the Buddhist point of view and should be resisted. Buddhism is very individualistic in the sense that Buddhists believe that individuals should use their own lives to their own full evolutionary benefit.

When we come to the guru relationship in Buddhism, because of that individualism, the teacher relationship is not very strong in mainstream Buddhism, monastic Buddhism, Mahayana Buddhism, or social Buddhism. Buddhism was critical of the Indian authoritarian patriarchal guru. Instead, Buddhists have a concept of a spiritual friend who acts as an example. He helps us bring out our potential; it's not just indoctrination. On the Tantric level of Buddhism, when we go through the unconscious and get into our archetypes, then the guru thing comes back into play in the form of using the lama as an icon for our transference. There is the concept of initiation, and we have to practice visualizing our teacher, or lama, as if that lama were Buddha. And in that sense, we make an icon out of a living being. The Tantric component of Tibetan Buddhism gets into that issue very deeply, and the lama relationship becomes all-important. It is a relationship that requires a delicate balance. On the one hand, we do a practice where we see no fault in the guru, and at the same time we use all our critical energy on ourselves in order to transform ourselves and realize *our* Buddha potential.

❖❖❖

EPILOGUE

It is important to know what is occurring in Tibet. This knowledge will help us better understand what is happening here in our own culture. Buddhism offers us some insights and reflections that can give us more clarity about ourselves and the world around us. This is not a new religion to adopt because it's better. Rather, it's an opportunity for us to expand our horizons and become more tolerant, whatever our spiritual persuasion may be. Take the principles presented within these pages, and adapt them to your spiritual path; use what works and discard the rest. Know that the Buddha is within in the same way that God is within. Your life will be better for it. May these words be for the benefit of all beings everywhere.

❖❖❖ ❖❖❖

Appendix

RECOMMENDED READING

The Awakening of the West: The Encounter of Buddhism and Western Culture, by Stephen Batchelor

Awakening the Buddha Within: Eight Steps to Enlightenment, by Lama Surya Das

Awakening the Mind, Lightening the Heart, by His Holiness The Dalai Lama

Awakening the Sleeping Buddha, by Tai Situpa Rinpoche

Being Peace, by Thich Nhat Hanh

Buddha's Little Instruction Book, by Jack Kornfield

Buddhism Without Beliefs: A Contemporary Guide to Awakening, by Stephen Batchelor

Encouraging Words: Zen Buddhist Teachings for Western Students, by Robert Aitken

Enlightened Journey, by Tulku Thondup

Essential Tibetan Buddhism, by Robert A. F. Thurman

The Facts of Life from a Buddhist Perspective, by Lama Surya Das

The Faith to Doubt: Glimpses of Buddhist Uncertainty, by Stephen Batchelor

The Gateless Barrier, translated by Robert Aitken

The Ground We Share: Everyday Practice, Buddhist and Christian, by Robert Aitken and David Steindl-Rast

The Healing Power of Mind: Simple Meditation Exercises for Health, Well-Being, and Enlightenment, by Tulku Thondup

Inside Tibetan Buddhism: Rituals and Symbols Revealed, by Robert A. F. Thurman

Interbeing: Fourteen Guidelines for Engaged Buddhism, by Thich Nhat Hanh

The Joy of Living and Dying in Peace, by His Holiness The Dalai Lama

Living Buddha, Living Christ, by Thich Nhat Hanh

Living Dharma: Teachings of Twelve Buddhist Masters, by Jack Kornfield

Love in Action: Writings on Nonviolent Social Change, by Thich Nhat Hanh

Masters of Meditation and Miracles, by Tulku Thondup

Natural Great Perfection—Nyoshul Khenpo, translated by Lama Surya Das

Old Path White Clouds, by Thich Nhat Hanh

Original Dwelling Place: Zen Buddhist Essays, by Robert Aitken

A Path with Heart, by Jack Kornfield

Peace Is Every Step: The Path of Mindfulness in Everyday Life, by Thich Nhat Hanh

The Power of Compassion, by His Holiness The Dalai Lama

The Practice of Perfection, by Robert Aitken

Seeds of Peace, by Sulak Sivaraksa

The Snow Lion's Turquoise Mane: Wisdom Tales from Tibet, by Lama Surya Das

Teachings of the Buddha, edited by Jack Kornfield

The Tibetan Book of Living and Dying, by Soygal Rinpoche

The Tibetan Book of the Dead, translated by Robert A. F. Thurman

Violence & Compassion, by His Holiness The Dalai Lama

The Way to Freedom, by His Holiness The Dalai Lama

A Zen Wave: Basho's Haiku & Zen, by Robert Aitken

NEW DIMENSIONS AUDIOCASSETTES

These audiocassettes are the word-for-word recordings of the original radio conversations from which *Buddhism in the West* was compiled.

ZEN ETHICS, with **ROBERT AITKEN ROSHI**. How do we maintain personal integrity and grow spiritually in times of confusion and chaos? The answer to this question serves as the basis for an enlightening dialogue with an American *roshi*. Cutting through the materialism of contemporary society, Aitken Roshi speaks of ways to live with clarity and compassion. Contrary to the monastic tradition of giving up the world, he suggests that we can be active in the world while holding true to our own principles without compromise. Bringing the depth of the meditative experience to the challenges of everyday existence underscores this penetrating and relevant conversation. Aitken Roshi is the author of *Taking the Path of Zen* and *The Mind of Clover*.

Tape #1897   1 hr. $9.95

DHARMA WISDOM, with **KALU RINPOCHE**. One of the most respected teachers in Tibetan Buddhism, the late Venerable Kalu Rinpoche speaks to the relevance of Buddhist principles in modern contemporary life. His simplicity, clarity, and directness provide a thoughtful and enheartening message for the spirit. This is a rare dialogue with a sage of great wisdom and love who lived in a cave for 13 years.

Tape #2031   1 hr. $9.95

LOVINGKINDNESS AND ACTIVE PEACE, with **H. H. THE DALAI LAMA** and **H. E. TAI SITUPA**. Recipient of the 1989

Nobel Prize for Peace, the Dalai Lama has emerged as one of the great spiritual figures of this century. Here, in an exclusive interview with Michael Toms, he speaks of his positive impressions of Costa Rica, the purpose of religion, his memorable meeting with Thomas Merton, the individual's responsibility for change, and the relationship between Tibet and China. Further remarks were recorded during his visit to San Francisco in October 1989 as part of the Pilgrimage for Active Peace. In the second part of this program, H. E. Tai Situpa, the conceiver and organizer of the Pilgrimage, suggests ways to encourage compassion or the "good heart" and emphasizes the relevance of "active peace."

Tape #2157   1 hr. $9.95

EMBRACING LIFE THROUGH LOVINGKINDNESS, with **JACK KORNFIELD**. Every life brings suffering and setbacks. When life deals its most terrible blows, however, we also receive its greatest gift: We stop to consider the purpose of being human, and begin to discover what is important and meaningful in life. We learn compassion, which frees us from selfish confusion and allows us to act simply and effectively. What Buddhists call "lovingkindness" begins to find an opening into our lives. And it is in the midst of our everyday distractions and concerns that this principle becomes most meaningful. Hear about how this truly can happen in our own lives, in the words of one of the most beloved and well-known teachers of Vipassana Buddhism. Presented here is not only inspiration that brings out the deep "yes" from our hearts, but practical advice for how to carry out this inspiration to heal our daily life. And, as Kornfield reminds us, "The healing of ourselves is the same as the healing of the world." He is a founder of the Insight Meditation Society and the author of *A Path With Heart* and *Buddha's Little Instruction Book*.

Tape #2452   1 hr. $9.95

BUDDHISM: PAST, PRESENT, AND FUTURE, with **STEPHEN BATCHELOR**. Whether you have an interest in Buddhism—or whether you are completely confused by its complexity—here is a highly illuminating overview of the history and character of Buddhism throughout the world. Batchelor traces the historical cultural cross-currents that carried it through India, China, and Tibet; into ancient Greece, Europe, and the modern Western world—including his own life experiences in Zen and Tibetan Buddhism. In the process, there arises a clear definition of just what Buddhism is—its strengths, weaknesses, and central aims. "Buddhism addresses the immediacy of your own experience," says Batchelor. . . .It's concerned with freeing the mind, about reducing suffering in the world." He is a renowned Buddhist teacher and scholar, and the author of several books, including *The Awakening of the West*.

Tape #2504   1 hr. $9.95

BASIC BUDDHIST WISDOM, with **THICH NHAT HANH**. Thich Nhat Hanh is one of the foremost teachers of Buddhism in the West, and here he explores Buddhism, Christianity, the concepts of soul, impermanence, mindfulness, and much more. "Everything is impermanent," he says. "Not only is your body impermanent, but your feelings, your perceptions, your mental formations, your consciousness also. . . . Instead of complaining that things are impermanent, we have to welcome impermanence as a factor to make life possible—Long Live Impermanence!" Nominated for the Nobel Peace Prize by Martin Luther King, Jr., during the Vietnam War, Thich Nhat Hanh is the author of many books, including *Living Buddha, Living Christ* and *Cultivating the Mind of Love: The Practice of Looking Deeply in the Mahayana Buddhist Tradition*.

Tape #2545   1 hr. $9.95

SCHLEPPING TOWARD ENLIGHTENMENT, with LAMA SURYA DAS. A Jewish lama from New York gives us a modern American update on the Eastern spiritual wisdom to which he has dedicated his life since the '60s. His gentle humor and sincerity sparkle through the hard reminders that "if it doesn't show up in life as common sense, as sagacity, as sanity, what good is it?" He emphasizes "bringing the dharma home" to our daily life, so that whatever our spiritual belief or practice may be, it will be relevant "through and through our whole life." A worthy challenge calling us back to truth and integrity in everyday life. "If it's not here," asks Surya Das, "where would it be?" He is founder of the Dzogchen Foundation in Cambridge, Massachusetts; and author of *The Snow Lion's Turquoise Mane* and co-author of *Natural Great Perfection* and *Awakening the Buddha Within: Timeless Teachings from Tibet.*

Tape #2571   1 hr. $9.95

IT'S ALL IN YOUR MIND, with LAMA TULKU THONDUP RINPOCHE. Rinpoche draws on his early childhood in Tibet traveling with his nomadic parents, followed by years of classical education of Buddhism in a Tibetan monastery. He had to rely on the goodness of others when forced to leave his homeland after the Chinese invasion and relocate to India, learn a new language and new skills. He speaks with authority about how problems can be opportunities to strengthen peace and compassion in our lives and help us grow spiritually. Lama Tulku Thondup tells us that even when a situation is bad, when you blame others for it, you create hatred in yourself. He says, "This hatred will create more stress and pressure. . . .You will become like a burning hell." Rinpoche also speaks about how peace and joy are a product of the mind: "We must use the mind to improve and heal our life." He suggests four specific tools as powerful exercises for improving our lives. A former visiting scholar at Harvard University, Rinpoche has written many books, including *Master of Meditation and Miracles, Enlightened Journey,* and *The Healing Power of Mind: Simple Mediation Exercises for Health, Well-Being, and Enlightenment.*

Tape #2607   1 hr. $9.95

TIBETAN WISDOM FOR THE WEST with **ROBERT THURMAN**. More than 1.3 million Tibetans have lost their lives, and over 6,000 monasteries have been destroyed since the Chinese invasion in 1949. One of the positive legacies amidst this tragic story is the release of the Tibetan Buddhist spiritual wisdom, hidden for thousands of years deep in the Himalayas. Robert Thurman believes this legacy is meant for you and me, now, here in America, as we struggle with the lack of meaning inherent in a materialistic society. He envisions the possibility of a "tremendous worldwide renaissance" if "enough of us can take the hint of the emergency nature of our present world system and the unviability of the material, industrial machinery." Thurman is the chair at the Department of Religion at Columbia University, and president of The Tibet House in New York, a cultural and educational institution that he co-founded with actor Richard Gere. He is also the author of several books on Tibet, including *Wisdom and Compassion: The Sacred Art of Tibet, The Central Philosophy of Tibet,* and *Essential Tibetan Buddhism.*

Tape #2619   1 hr. $9.95

TO ORDER TAPES

Call toll-free (800) 935-8273. Each tape is $9.95 unless otherwise noted, plus postage, shipping, and handling.

BOOKS, AUDIOS, AND MORE
FROM NEW DIMENSIONS FOUNDATION
(available through Hay House)

Books

Buddhism in the West—The Dalai Lama and other contributors
Money, Money, Money—Jacob Needleman and other contributors
The Power of Meditation and Prayer—Larry Dossey, M.D., and other
    contributors
Roots of Healing—Andrew Weil, M.D., and other contributors
The Soul of Business—Charles Garfield and other contributors
The Well of Creativity—Julia Cameron and other contributors

Audios

(All of the audios below feature New Dimensions Radio co-founder Michael Toms interviewing some of the foremost thinkers and social innovators of our time.)

The Art of Soul Work—Thomas Moore
Authentic Power—Gary Zukav
Future Medicine—Daniel Goleman
Healing from the Inside Out—Bernie Siegel, M.D.
Healing with Spirit—Caroline Myss, Ph.D.
The Heart of Spiritual Practice—Jack Kornfield
Live Long and Feel Good—Andrew Weil, M.D.
Make Your Dreams Real—Barbara Sher
Making Magic in the World—Maya Angelou
Medicine, Meaning, and Prayer—Larry Dossey, M.D.
Messages of the Celestine Prophecy—James and Salle Redfield
A New Approach to Medicine—Andrew Weil, M.D.
The New Millennium—Jean Houston
Psychic and Intuitive Healing—Barbara Brennan, Rosalyn Bruyere, and Judith
    Orloff
Roots of Healing—Andrew Weil, M.D., and others
Sacred Odyssey—Ram Dass
The Wisdom of Joseph Campbell—Joseph Campbell

Calendar

Wise Words: Perennial Wisdom from the New Dimensions Radio Series

(To order the products above, please call Hay House at 800-654-5126.)

NEW DIMENSIONS FOUNDATION

Since its inception in 1973, New Dimensions Foundation has presented lecture series, live events, and seminars; published books, sponsored educational tours, and launched a major periodical. Created to address the dramatic cultural shifts and changing human values in our society, New Dimensions has become an international forum for some of the most innovative ideas expressed on the planet. Its principal and best-known activity is New Dimensions Radio, an independent producer of radio dialogues and other programming.

During the past 20 years, many of this century's leading thinkers and social innovators have spoken through New Dimensions. The programming supports a diversity of views from many traditions and cultures. Now is a time for transformative learning and for staying open to all possibilities. We must constantly be willing to review and revise what we are creating. New Dimensions fosters the goals of living a more healthy life of mind, body, and spirit while deepening our connections to self, family, community, environment, and planet.

New Dimensions is a rare entity in the world of media—a completely independent, noncommercial radio producer. Primary support comes from listeners. Members of "Friends of New Dimensions" (FOND) are active partners in a community of hope and grounded optimism as we celebrate the human spirit and explore new ideas, provocative insights, and creative solutions across the globe over the airwaves.

You too can play an invaluable part in this positive force for change by becoming a member of (FOND) and supporting the continued production and international distribution of New Dimensions Radio programming.

Become a Member of FOND

As a Member of "Friends of New Dimensions" (FOND), you will receive:

- The *New Dimensions Journal,* a bimonthly magazine containing captivating articles, reviews of books, video and audio tapes, current "New Dimensions" program schedules, selections of audio tapes from our archives, and much more.

- The New Dimensions Annual Tape Catalog and periodic supplements.

- A 15% discount on any product purchased through New Dimensions, including books, New Dimensions tapes, and selected tapes from other producers.

- A quality thank-you gift expressing our deepest appreciation.

- The satisfaction of knowing that you are supporting the broadcast of hopeful visions to people all across the nation and the world.

Contributions are tax deductible to the extent allowed by law. With Visa, Mastercard, or Discover, please call (800) 935-8273.

A nonprofit tax-exempt educational organization
P.O. Box 569 • Ukiah, CA 95482 • 707-468-5215
*Website: **www.newdimensions.org** • E-mail: **ndradio@igc.org***

❖❖❖

We hope you enjoyed
this Hay House/New Dimensions book.
If you would like to receive a free catalog featuring additional
Hay House books and products, or if you would like
information about the Hay Foundation,
please contact:

Hay House, Inc.
P.O. Box 5100
Carlsbad, CA 92018-5100

(760) 431-7695 or (800) 654-5126
(760) 431-6948 (fax) or (800) 650-5115 (fax)

Please visit the Hay House Website at:
www.hayhouse.com
and the New Dimensions Website at:
www.newdimensions.org

❖❖❖